CONTROL + ALT + DELETE

*"Soft Boot" your personal operating system
and enhance your leadership success!*

RALPH HOWARD

Brian –
Welcome to the PFI Board.
I Hope you enjoy the Book!

RALPH

PARKE PRESS
Norfolk, Virginia

Control + Alt + Delete Leadership

ISBN 978-0-9843339-2-9

Published by Parke Press, Norfolk, Virginia • www.parkepress.com

Library of Congress Control Number is available upon request

Printed in the United States of America

CONTENTS

PREFACE

This book is written for aspiring and advancing professionals looking for a simplistic model to follow for leadership, supported with inspiring stories of business success. But they won't be stories from the highly over-publicized *public* company leaders of today. There are no quotes, or conversations with Jack Welch, Jeffrey Immelt, or any of the other giants of public business. Their stories are well chronicled, and readily available at your local Barnes and Noble. Rather, I'll introduce you to some really excellent leaders from within the world of *privately*-held businesses.

By their very nature, it's difficult to garner a view into the realm of private business today. I've had the good fortune of working within two blue-chip private companies in my career (Kohler Company and Pella Windows and Doors), and I'll introduce you to some of the stellar leaders I've had the pleasure of working with – and share with you some intriguing aspects of leadership and business success. And along the way, we'll spend some time exploring that ever elusive concept of work/life balance.

Is it really possible to have a successful career in the chaotic dog-eat-dog world of business today while maintaining the sanity and sanctity you desire and need from your personal life? You bet it is. It starts by setting

1

a clear course for yourself, remaining focused on what's really important, and not allowing yourself to become derailed from your goals. The *Control + Alt + Delete* framework I'll share with you in this book will help you sort through what's important to *you*, and put in place a structure that will get you to think about your path on a daily basis – and any course corrections you may need to take to keep yourself on track against your goals for success, individuality, perspective and balance.

Control + Alt + Delete. Three simple key strokes most of us use in concert as we begin our work days by booting up our computers. Key strokes used to "soft boot" these electronic instruments – electrifying the brains within these machines to carry out our biddings in supporting our 21st century business and life activities.

At its very essence, the computer is a device built on a foundation of *logic*, given to it by man. So, too, is it possible that we can take back a little bit of that simple logic from the computer and use it as a daily reminder of how to give our careers and lives a "soft boot" as well?

What you will get from reading this book is the framework that I've built for myself as my career has taken me from being an engineering graduate in 1985 to running Canac Cabinets – a multi-national Kohler Company business that employed over 1,900 associates across the U.S. and Canada. At its simplest form, consider the following:

Control. *You* are responsible for your own professional and personal development. You...and nobody else. Control smartly what you can, and have the perspective to recognize that there is much you cannot control.

Alt. The "Alt" key is a modifier key. Alternatives and options are good things. Be an agent of change, and make course corrections and needed modifications on a regular and consistent basis.

Delete. In business and in life, it's critical to recognize the things that can derail you and keep you from achieving your goals. Recognize them – and deal with them decisively.

So we'll begin now and explore the *Contol + Alt + Delete* model in noteworthy detail. I'm confident that everyone who reads this book will take from it some valuable nuggets that you can put into application immediately. My hope is that when you come to pause down the road and gaze into your personal satisfaction mirror – you'll like the reflection of yourself that you see!

INTRODUCTION

This book is divided into three sections. True to the *Control + Alt + Delete* framework, the first section lays out the elements and structure by which to sort through what's important to you as you develop your career and your leadership characteristics. The *Control* section.

Fundamental to the *Control* section is recognizing that *you* are responsible for your own development...you and nobody else! It's about self-management, and self-management begins with self-awareness. It's about being aware of your professional and personal environment, and their relative consistency with your individual goals. It's about introspection and leading first with positive character.

What do you stand for? And importantly – what do you want your legacy to be? As we develop as leaders, we are often times looked to for guidance – and yes – even for making decisions! And this is where self-awareness and character screens become so critical.

Decisions are typically *not* independent – rather they are interdependent. In a business environment, Strategy/ Organization / and People are all interconnected. Changing one usually will affect the others. In Section 1, we'll have a look at some defining characteristics of

leaders – both good and bad – and I'll introduce you to
"The Four Controls of Business Leadership." These
controls will help you navigate your career on a daily
basis, and they will help you develop your professional and
personal "peripheral vision."

The second section of this book explores the concepts of
"Alt" and *"Delete."* After spending some important time in
leadership and character introspection, it's time to take a
look at managed change.

In both business and in life, there is often more than
one right answer. More than one path you can choose
to achieve a desired result. As long as you achieve your
desired result, does the path you take to get there really
matter? Does the end justify the means?

As a leader, it's important to have peripheral vision.
Others may take issue with this view, and they may
espouse the importance of having "tunnel vision" – just
keeping your eyes on the prize. How you get there *does*
matter, and leaders of character recognize the importance
of proper path.

As you climb the corporate ladder, whom are you leaving
behind?

The third and final section of this book explores the
concept of work/life balance. In part, it's a personal
treatise of things the author has experienced and learned
along his professional journey – and candidly - many
things were learned the hard way.

To be clear – Dr. Phil I'm not. Nor do I pretend to be.
Along my personal journey, I've left a wake of failed
marriages, as my drive for professional success took on
a very high priority for me. Setting high standards is a

valued competency in business, and it should carry equal weight in your personal life. That's the *balance* part that so often gets lost in the shuffle.

Sharing a common vision, and having regular communication around that vision, assures alignment and allows you to *"Alt"* changes as needed. This holds true both at work and at home. As simple a concept as it sounds, so often we find ourselves totally spent by the time we get home, that we give our significant others and families what little is left over, rather than what they truly deserve. And all too often, we let the tug-of-war between our business lives and our personal lives rage on during the few hours we have each day with our beloved families.

Technology has enabled us to carry our business weapons right into our own homes – further stacking the deck against personal sanctity and fulfillment. Undisciplined use of cell phones, PDA's, and wifi-enabled laptops is stripping away at the quality time that should be spent with family and friends, and on personal enrichment.

Getting and keeping that important work/life balance is not all that complicated, but it does require discipline. SELF discipline. Your wife, children, or significant others are your personal "Board of Directors." They should be listened to with a keen ear, and their views, interests and guidance must be considered and respected accordingly.

SECTION 1
The Four Controls of Business Leadership

Control + Alt + Delete. Most of us recognize these three keystrokes as a command to "soft boot" our computers. David Bradley, a designer who worked on the original IBM PC, chose this combination so that both hands are required to help prevent *accidentally* rebooting. Seeking out these three unique keys forces one to stop and THINK for a moment.

We typically find ourselves depressing this sequence on two occasions. The first is in the morning after we've hustled to work, washed down a glazed doughnut with an overpriced "grande skinny latte," and settled into our offices... usually about 10 minutes later than intended. The work day has just started, and we're already "chasin' it."

Late for school... again

Instead of shaking hands with the clock, we end up arm wrestling with it throughout our day. Now there's NO TIME for the "luxury" of stopping and thinking because we're already behind. It's like the little boy who arrived late, panting and sweating after briskly walking his bike to school. When the teacher asked why he didn't ride the

9

bike, he replied, "I was so late, I didn't have the time to stop and get on it."

The point of this book is to help you "get on," and overcome – or at least challenge – the kind of thinking (or lack thereof) that is keeping you sweaty, exhausted, and late for school. It's about making sure you achieve a passing grade in leadership and career development – as well as relationship satisfaction – because you've actively participated in class and you've smartly done your homework.

While your computer is bringing up its operating system in the morning, you can give thought to the *Control + Alt + Delete* model and energize your *own* operating system as well.

Three simple keys. Three simple, yet powerful, thoughts. That's the premise of this book.

As Albert Einstein once said, "Any intelligent fool can make things bigger, more complex... it takes a touch of genius – and a lot of courage – to move in the opposite direction." Sage counsel. So... no three-dimensional flow charts... no external forces modeling... no litany of business school buzz words... and no slick four-letter acronyms. Just common speak. Common speak, and common sense – as uncommon as that might be.

"Keys" to organization

Control. *You* are responsible for your own professional and personal development. You... and nobody else. Control smartly what you can, and have the perspective to recognize that there is much you cannot control.

Alt. The "Alt" key is a modifier key. Alternatives and options are good things. Be an agent of change, and make course corrections and neecessary modifications on a regular and consistent basis.

Delete. In business and in life, it's critical to recognize the things that can derail you from achieving your goals. Recognize them – and deal with them decisively.

Stop digging

The second occasion to strike the *Control + Alt + Delete* key combination on your computer is when something has gone awry. (These keys are sometimes referred to as "interrupt keys", since they can be used to interrupt the operation of a malfunctioning program.)

When things start to go haywire for you – either professionally or personally – invoke your own "interrupt keys." In other words, when you find yourself in a hole – the first thing you should do is STOP DIGGING. Then use the three rungs on the *Control + Alt + Delete* ladder to help you climb out and get yourself back on course.

The essential relevance of the *Control + Alt + Delete* model begins with recognizing that there is often more than one right answer; more than one valid path you can choose. Leaders of character recognize this, and they invest quality time and energy in understanding the *implications* of their decisions, and hence the importance of choosing the best road.

Companies, businesses and organizations are woven of the key structural fibers of strategy, structure and people. When you make a change to one of these threads, **11** it usually impacts the other two. Leaders of character recognize this, and they think through the implications of making a change BEFORE they put the change into motion.

That's ready/aim/fire... not ready/fire/aim

Right smack dab in the middle of "**life**," you'll find "if." Skilled leaders recognize that *probability* is much more prevalent in the daily course than *certainty*. Knowing this, they hone their skills at being able to understand and *Control* probability as best they can.

Some would call it "peripheral vision," and we all have it to some degree. Whether it's an innate ability or not, it is something that can be learned and refined, using the *Control + Alt + Delete* model as your guide.

Follow me: Three leadership styles

Think for a moment about the leaders you've come across during your life – and not just in your professional career. These might be anyone from your den master in Cub Scouts, to the captain of your high school football team or cheerleading squad, to the leader of your church or Kiwanis Club (and yes – it may even include parent(s)!) Each has taught you some meaningful leadership lessons; that's why you remember them.

As you reflect, try to quantify them based on these categories:

High-Quality Leaders
Peripheral vision skills
Strong, positive character
Belief that success comes from the team
Good communicator
Genuine
Connected and predictable

Ho-Hum Leaders
Non-descript
Task masters
Blind spots in self-awareness
Lacking in vision

Posers
Cloaked in executive camouflage
Lack authenticity
Book-of-the-month managers
Image trumps substance
Professional parasites

My own tallies came out something like this:

High Quality Leaders	=	10 percent
Ho-Hum Leaders	=	70 percent
Posers	=	20 percent

Growing up in the heartland of America (Wisconsin Dells, Wisconsin) I was fortunate to have been raised in a household with parents who both exhibited what I consider to be high-quality leadership. They were school teachers and active in the community, so I got to see them apply their leadership skills outside as well as inside the family.

Both demonstrated consistency. They were good communicators, and they were uncompromising when it came to issues of integrity and character. Not only were they effective individually, but they worked together successfully in the partnership of marriage, and, in fact, just celebrated their 52nd wedding anniversary. Not many can claim a track record like that! Including their offspring... (I just celebrated my own 10-year anniversary of sorts this past year. Unfortunately, it took me three different wives to rack up my 10 years of marriage – but more on that later.)

Profile of a high-quality leader – Coach Fred Kuhl

One of the high-quality leaders from my youth was Coach Fred Kuhl. He was my high school physical education teacher and head football coach of the Wisconsin Dells Chiefs. He was also the leader of our Fellowship of Christian Athletes chapter, which gave us further insight into the man and his makeup.

Coach Kuhl led the team to a number of conference championships, but just as importantly, he positively guided the lives of many of his students and players. He was consistent and demanding in his expectations of us, a strong communicator, and he surrounded himself with assistants who exhibited many of the same qualities that he had.

Coach Kuhl was tough on the practice field, and yet we would see his more diplomatic side when we would go to his home on Monday nights to watch game film from the previous Friday. He was exacting, yet fair in all his assessments. In other words, he was well balanced between his head, his heart, and his hands. Consequently, he successfully maximized the talents of a band of average athletes – allowing a small school to win out over much larger schools in our conference – with arguably better athletes.

Clear direction. High expectations. An accurate, reliable moral compass, and hands-on in his teaching. These were his hallmarks. He taught us the value of getting to know your team at a deeper level than just executing the task at hand, and letting them get to know and understand *you*.

The Coach Kuhl lesson?

Press the flesh. Make it a point to learn something new about someone on your team every day, and be consistent in your leadership.

Detached leadership doesn't work. It's one of the important differentiators between High-Quality Leaders and the Ho-Hum. You can't be an inaccessible Wizard of Oz operating behind the curtain and expect to connect with – much less motivate – your team. The best leaders understand the importance of having strong interpersonal skills, including empathy, and having a knack for facilitating collaboration, cooperation and enthusiasm.

As a leader, *connecting with your team* brings with it the exponential value of better results through collective effort. That's because you have harnessed a team of *engaged associates* who function with a common sense of purpose and belonging.

I believe that *consistency* is an underappreciated quality of excellent leaders. As a leader, you need to be steady and unfailing, like a pilot light ready to ignite the fire within the organization. Consistent. Always on… and always ready.

Brett Favre, the recently departed quarterback and unquestioned leader of the Green Bay Packers for 16 years, was extremely skilled in this regard. In 2007, the Packers had the youngest football team in the NFL. And yet they played so well together that they fashioned a 13-3 regular season record, and were just one interception away from making a trip to Super Bowl XLII.

Although often unpredictable to his opposing teams, he was very predictable to his own. His young squad knew they could rely on his direction – regardless of what was happening on the field.

You need to know what *your team* will do in challenging situations, and they need to know what *you* will do as well. You shouldn't "sneak up" on them, or try to "keep them guessing." Predictability is critical to your team's performance.

Consequently, to be a consistent and "even" leader, you shouldn't be driven by "mood," but rather by those principals and fundamentals that are understood and accepted by the organization.

Ever wonder why when someone is considered "moody," the "mood" is always a bad one? Many otherwise effective leaders have fallen prey to their mood swings. "Better stay away from the boss today... he's in a lousy mood. Maybe I'll try her again tomorrow, or send an email instead." If only they were aware and had the discipline to *Control* acting on the impulses of passing emotion!

Noted sociologist Charles Horton Cooley suggests: "Form the habit of making decisions when your spirit is fresh ... to let dark moods lead is like choosing cowards to command armies."

16

If you're over the age of three, mood can, and should be, controlled. High-quality leaders recognize this and they *Control* their demeanor for the good of the team (and they *Alt* as needed in private.) Predictable, consistent, effective and connected.

Fee, fie... Ho-hum

The valley of the Ho-Hum is a land of non-descript, mildly-effective leaders. Unfortunately, it's an expansive valley with scores of professional residents. By simple count, I would say that about 70 percent of managers or leaders fall into this category.

Some of these might be considered "task masters." Not particularly strong leaders, but they do move forward steadily to the monotonous, regular beat of the drum, carrying out the busy work of the day. Often these folks were thrust into their roles with little or no training on how to be a good manager, much less an effective leader. (It's not an indictment against them, but against the majority of organizations that don't offer the proper training and skills development.)

Most people enter the business world in an "individual contributor" role. A salesperson. An engineer. An accountant. With a little luck, hard work and dedication, we advance to the next levels. Senior salesperson. Senior engineer. Senior accountant. They typically advance because they've built a record of success.

Then they're promoted to first-line management positions. Branch sales manager. Engineering manager. Manager of cost accounting. But being a good accountant doesn't mean the individual will be a good accounting *manager*.

Most people are familiar with the "Peter Principle" – an idea first formulated by Canadian author Laurence J. Peter in his best-selling book *The Peter Principle: Why Things Always Go Wrong* (1969). The central thesis of Peter's satirical commentary on business bureaucracies is that "in a hierarchy, every employee tends to rise to his level of incompetence."

They move up within the organization until they get into a role where they have limited success – often not because of lack of ability – but rather due to improper *application* of their abilities.

Leadership needs to be developed. It's not a position, and you don't magically acquire the necessary qualities because you are promoted into a position with a title that says so.

Plumbing the depths of talent: Leadership development at Kohler Co.

One blue-chip American company built on its success by understanding the Peter Principle and the futility of "typical business promotion practice." It prepares its young leaders for success *before* promoting them to crucial leadership positions.

From its very beginning in 1873, the story of Kohler Company is all about embracing opportunity. Through the years, the company – its leadership and the skilled associates who toil in its offices and factories – has pursued a mission devoted to extending "higher levels of gracious living" to its customers. Consequently, Kohler Company is the recognized global leader in kitchen and bath products. As one of the largest privately-held companies in the United States, Kohler has also built a position of global leadership in products and services outside of the kitchen and bath, including power systems, interiors, and hospitality.

I've had the privilege to work for Kohler twice in my career, beginning in the late 1980's, returning again in 2001 to help lead the repositioning and integration of *Sterling* brand plumbing into what became "Plumbing Americas."

The plumbing business of Kohler Company in the Americas is made up of three brands (*Figure 1*): The *Sterling* brand, which is positioned primarily as a trade brand, protects *Kohler* brand from attack from the lower-price side of the market. *Sterling's* kitchen and bath products are functionally innovative, and priced in the economy to mid-price ranges.

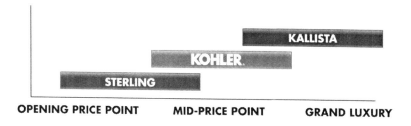

Figure 1: Kohler's North American brand positioning

Kohler brand occupies the coveted middle ground, and has earned its premier market position through time-honored, uncompromising commitment to their customers' needs, and by bringing "aspirational qualities" to its products for the *middle* of the market.

The third brand in the portfolio is *Kallista. Kallista* products are "grand-luxury" in design and priced accordingly. These product designs span from delightfully

19

classic, to edgy contemporary, appealing to interior designers and their discriminating customers.

Upon completion of my first assignment back at Kohler Company with *Sterling*, I became vice president of sales for Plumbing Americas. After a long and focused search to find the right person to drive training and development of our multi-national sales force, we were fortunate to find Doug Dillon, a fine example of leadership "done right."

Doug came to us fresh from the telecommunications industry where he had demonstrated impressive leadership and performance management, as well as proven sales success. His first order of business at Kohler was to assess the capabilities and needs of our team.

In keeping with his reputation, Doug brought much-needed structure and enhancement to our basic knowledge and skills training curriculum. But it's what he did beyond "the expected" that took our manager effectiveness to the "next level," and netted us a "best practice" recognition by the Sales Executive Council (the sales leadership arm of the highly-regarded Corporate Executive Board).

Mapping the territory

The process Doug initiated involved defining the characteristics of our high-performing sales associates versus those of our core performers, and did the same with our sales managers. With the assistance of the Sales Executive Council (SEC), we "mapped out" our sales team to determine how/where our core performers invested their time, and how/where those schedules deviated from those of our high performers.

Doug took *Control* of this complicated initiative, and he was able to generate great enthusiasm for it among the sales management team with the skilled application of *indirect influence.* (Recognizing and valuing indirect influence is one of **The Four Controls of Business Leadership,** *p. 35.*) In essence, he helped the team truly understand the long-term value we would derive from this effort and not dismiss or resent it as an extraneous corporate exercise.

The results were impactful.

From this exercise, we developed a set of protocols and tools to enable the core group to more closely emulate the activities of our highest performers. We eliminated time-wasting "busy work" that is the bane of every sales rep, and redirected their efforts to more effective call planning and preparation.

For managers, we put an emphasis on three critical "star performer" qualities:
1. Effective, team-based deployment of planning and strategy.
2. Increased support to the most important aspects of the sale – the initial presentation, and closing the deal.
3. Increased emphasis on coaching, mentoring and developing teams.

These tools enabled us to better *Control* our probability for success. The next challenge was how to increase the probability of harnessing the right management **talent.**

New heights with "Top Gun"

Top Gun was the result – a program to better identify "the best of the best" solutions-ready manager candidates – and to prepare them BEFORE placing them into crucial management/leadership positions.

Here's how it works:

To identify solutions-ready manager candidates from our sales rep pool, we introduced a series of prequalifications to screen for eligibility based on historical job performance and a preliminary assessment of potential. This was a three-phase process:

Phase 1 – Preliminary manager competency screening. We analyzed those reps that displayed strong sales performance (historically) and demonstrated daily behaviors that aligned with those of our successful managers. Twice each year, sales management staff identified candidates for Phase 2 screening.

Phase 2 – In-depth testing. This five-hour screening included both a written exam and a formal interview. The written exam probed for analytical reasoning, logic, quantitative skills, human relations understanding, energy and drive and emotional responsiveness – among other managerial abilities. The interview explored the candidate's career aspirations, strengths and potential (areas of development), using off-the-shelf assessment tools with "history," offering predictive characteristics around key successful manager attributes.

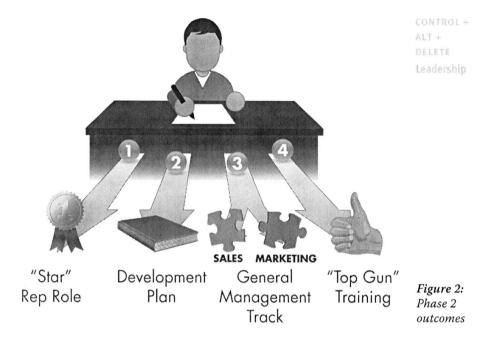

"Star" Rep Role	Development Plan	General Management Track	"Top Gun" Training

Figure 2:
Phase 2
outcomes

Following Phase 2, there are four possible outcomes (*Figure 2*):

1. Candidates are *not* considered managerial timbre and are redirected back into "individual contributor roles." Not to be undervalued or diminished, these candidates often became "star" salespeople.

2. Candidates have unrealized potential based on significant skill gaps. Such candidates were reviewed again following completion of targeted skills training.

3. Candidates who met the criteria for a general management track were moved laterally into roles *outside of sales* to gain experience in areas like marketing and supply-chain management.

4. Candidates were accepted into the "Top Gun" manager training program.

Phase 3 – Enrollment into the "Top Gun" manager training program. Top Gun is a 10-module training curriculum that covers topics such as business acumen, talent selection, people management, negotiation and coaching, among others. Each candidate designs a unique development plan, based on his or her personal assessment of strengths and weaknesses, along with input from the candidate's manager. They then present their development plans to their "Top Gun" classmates for collective review.

Throughout the one-year program, candidates apply solutions-management skills they have learned. Graduation requires a comprehensive presentation to classmates, training and development staff, as well as a presentation to the senior leadership team that outlines compliance and completion of their self-directed plan.

Many of these graduates went on to successful management careers. And because the program offered a thorough and realistic view of what management entails, some candidates (happily) chose to remain in individual sales rep roles. (This was a good thing. Instead of placing these people into management roles and watching them crash and burn, the "Top Gun" program enriched their understanding *ahead of time,* which prevented costly promotional missteps. This fostered a more successful and engaged workforce at every level.) See *Figure 3.*

Such a simple concept, and yet few companies actually prepare and equip their leaders for what is usually their most difficult career step – moving from being an *individual contributor* to being a *manager of people.*

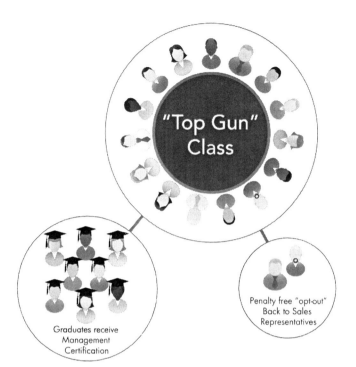

Figure 3:
"Top Gun"
outcomes

"Marshalling" the Dillon lesson

Doug is a genuine and articulate leader, and an excellent teacher. He has a unique knack for helping people with self-assessment, and he forms *trusting, connected relationships* with the "Top Gun" students. He skillfully uses indirect influence to gain engagement and support for his initiatives. And it pays off for "the company he keeps." Already, the impact of this program has skewed Kohler's management ranks toward quality leadership, steadily draining the Ho-Hum Manager "pool."

Pos-ing a problem??

As the name suggests, Posers are something other than what meets the eye. On the tame end of the poser scale is **25** the "book-of-the-month managers." They lack authenticity, bedrock values and skills, so they tend to remake themselves on a regular basis.

"By the book"...or buy the book?

Before settling into seat 21-B on her flight to Phoenix, she'll run into the airport book store and grab a copy of the latest top-selling business book to keep her company on her flight. She'll thumb through the pages, looking for the latest leadership model that worked at GE or P&G, in hopes that if she copies it, she, too, will become a leadership maven. So the next chance she gets with her team, she spews out some new buzz words to her co-workers...maybe puts a new "model" from the book into action...and proceeds to further damage her professional posture and ability to lead her team.

When this doesn't work, she reads *another* business book... from a *different* author... with *better* buzz words... *better* models...and so it goes, with more incarnations than Madonna or John Travolta.

This is not to disparage in any way the valuable nuggets that one can garner from the many fine books available on business success or leadership. Rather, it's to highlight the need to retain and develop *your own* individuality, and to encourage you to focus on honing your bedrock beliefs and skills, versus wasting time learning superficial techniques, supported with a new diction of jargon and superlatives.

Remoras and other slippery eels

More pernicious – often deadly – are the "professional parasites." These managers are self-centered, and they suck energy and life from teams and businesses for personal gain. Here, image always trumps substance. Sizzle is primary; steak is secondary. They have soufflé-like personal structure – puffed up on the outside and mushy on the inside. They progress through their careers cloaked in executive camouflage, concealing their own ineptness and taking credit for the successes of others. They are also quick to toss blame around like a clown tossing penny candy to children at a circus parade. Satirist Ambrose Bierce once defined responsibility as, "A detachable burden easily shifted to the shoulders of God, fate, fortune, luck, or one's neighbor. In the days of astrology it was customary to unload it upon a star." (I submit this quote as proof that professional parasites were thriving even back in the 1800's!)

Some professional parasites engage in downright malfeasance, but most do not. The majority work just inside the limits of the system, and they move on to their next victim organization before they are exposed at their current workplace. These are professional job jumpers, and they usually spend between 12 and 36 months at a company before disengaging with their current host organization and latching onto the next.

Locking in the lessons from Master Lock

Master Lock is a unit of publicly-traded conglomerate Fortune Brands. Based in the inner city of Milwaukee, Master Lock is the world's largest padlock manufacturer, selling over 50 million locks each year. They have also built up an amazing 97 percent consumer brand awareness over time with their target market.

Many of you of baby boomer age will likely recall the "bullet through the padlock" TV ads that were run during Super Bowls in the 70's and 80's. Master Lock debuted their simple 30-second "marksman" ad in 1974, demonstrating the durability of its product. A close-up of the shot padlock showed that the lock was able to withstand the impact of a rifle bullet and remain intact. The ad was extremely successful as it presented a very basic premise, supported with powerful and memorable imagery. The ad ran, with only slight variations, during the next 21 Super Bowls, and earned a legitimate and enviable position in advertising lore and history. (Those of you who don't recall the ads (perhaps younger Gen Xers or Gen Yers), no doubt will remember seeing the company name several times each day on your school locker.)

I joined Master Lock in 1992 as a product manager for the Door Hardware Division. It was there that I encountered one of my favorite leaders of excellence, along with three remarkably poisonous professional parasites.

Let's start with the good guy first.

Jim Beardsley was president and CEO when I arrived at Master Lock. He was the consummate professional, and he personified the sterling characteristics of a high-quality leader. He was principled, articulate, and he connected with employees throughout the organization.

He made a significant impression on me during my interview...but it's what *followed* that interview that was most impactful for me. We left Jim's office and we took a walk through the plant. (Master Lock had over 1,100 employees in Milwaukee, and the plant was unionized and

28

represented by the United Auto Workers.) The connection that Jim had with the employees and their fondness for him was evident. I'll never forget it.

The connected relationship "light bulb"

To a man and woman, they acknowledged him with smiles and greetings of respect – and he warmly reciprocated. He was courteous and respectful to all he encountered, with wonderful command of the three most powerful words in business...PLEASE and THANK YOU. Clearly he was leading a team that appreciated him and consequently enjoyed working for his company – not because they *had* to, but because they *wanted* to support him both as a professional and as an individual.

Listen up!

Jim was a very good strategist, which includes being an excellent listener. He "listened" with his ears *and* his eyes. He solicited and valued the opinions of others and never "talked over" the people within the organization. In turn, employees at every level listened intently when Jim spoke.

Jim had a terrific sense of proportion, which means he didn't speak unless he had something significant to say. To this day he stands in stark contrast to those who talk and endlessly pontificate as though paid by the word – carpeting the conference room with wall-to-wall words. These monologues fall on deaf ears. People tune out from the outset knowing it's too much work and frustration to find the core message buried within the rubble of yak.

American psychiatrist Karl Menninger once said;
"Listening is a magnetic and strange thing, a creative force.
The friends who listen to us are the ones we move toward,
and we want to sit in their radius. When we are listened
to, it creates us, makes us unfold and expand."

Jim's professional poise, structure, and executive
demeanor set him apart, and to this day, I've tried to
model *my* behavior around the way Jim carried himself,
and the respectful leadership he portrayed.

Master Lock under siege: 1992 to 1999

Before I introduce you to three wickedly-poisonous
professional parasites, let me provide you first with just a
bit more background on the state of affairs at Master Lock
at the time.

In the early part of my tenure (1992 to 1996), Master
Lock was on sound footing. We had strong margins, a
commanding market share position, and no branded
competitors. We were gaining traction in the market in
door hardware (which was a new category for us) and we
had sound leadership in place. Or so we thought.

Unfortunately, like many other American businesses in the
burgeoning 90's, we rather abruptly found ourselves under
heavy attack on multiple fronts.

Unlike the padlock business, the major players in door
hardware were units of well-financed, large corporate
conglomerates. Kwikset, the market share leader in the
category, was owned by Black & Decker. Schlage Lock, the
number two contender, was part of Ingersoll-Rand. And

Weiser Lock, the number three company, was part
of Masco.

As Master Lock began to gain share in the door hardware
category, the competition took notice, introducing new
products and developing metallic finishes that would
not tarnish or change color over time (among other
innovations). In addition, Black & Decker began to work
on a line of padlocks, competing with us in *our* core
business in the mass merchant and home center channels.
This was a crafty strategic play, forcing us to redirect funds
and organizational energy back to the padlock side of the
business to protect our position. (Ultimately, we sold off
the door hardware business altogether).

At the same time, manufacturers in China figured out how
to make padlocks equal to – and in some cases better than
– ours. Our manufacturing was done in Milwaukee, and
we were paying labor costs of almost $20 per hour (fully-
loaded) to produce our products there. China's labor cost
component was about 1/20th of that.

The mass-merchant retailers (Wal-Mart, Kmart, Target)
began allocating more shelf space to lower-cost Chinese
imports and their own house-brands (through which they
could enjoy richer margins).

Life as we had known it changed forever. We were under
siege from our domestic competitors, Chinese imports,
and even our own customers! We needed to craft our
turnaround strategy and execute it quickly and effectively
for both short-term survival and the long-term health of
the business.

If ever there was a time and need for strong leadership…
this was it. Unfortunately, a "siege mentality" also brings
the parasites to the fore like sharks to fresh blood in the

31

water. We had three of them and they were at high levels in the business. For purposes of our discussion, we'll refer to them as "Thing 1, Thing 2, and Thing 3."

Thing 1 was calculated and highly political. He was a master of unjust deception, and he never made a move without first asking the question – "What's in it for me?" He was a gifted public speaker, waxing poetically in front of groups – getting them to buy into his sort of religion – always passing the offering plate around so they could make a contribution to his cause.

He was a capable individual, but chose to apply himself in a self-centered fashion. Rather than providing real help in fixing the underpinnings of the business, he was busy playing his own game of "pin the tale on the president," undermining and looking to unseat Jim Beardsley at every turn.

And at the end of the day, he was ultimately successful in perpetuating the downward spiral of the business, and the eventual replacement of the president. Much to his chagrin, though, *he too* was replaced. His convoluted plan blew up in his face like a trick cigar. The best laid plans of mice, men and professional parasites!

Thing 2 was like Thing 1 in many ways. She, too, was all about style as opposed to substance, and she was always looking for the *personal* gain from her own actions and those of others. But she took it a step further. Where Thing 1 would operate just within the boundaries of the system, she crossed them. Cheating the system became modus operandi for her. With Thing 1 as her boss, she became "conditioned" to the idea that her parasitic actions were acceptable. Small indiscretions went unchecked, and larger ones followed, culminating in allegedly misdirecting co-op advertising moneys to bankroll an expensive athletic training program for herself and a few of her cronies. They would jet off to points unknown to climb mountains, whitewater raft, and train on mountain bikes. She was eventually exposed and removed from her position, but the damage was done.

And then there was Thing 3. Although also a professional parasite, he was different from the other two. Where they had abilities applied in bad form, Thing 3 was short on capability to begin with. Both Thing 1 and Thing 2 were skilled orators, and calculated in their speech and actions. Thing 3 was professionally aloof, and he would babble on like a fool in a barber's chair in company meetings and with customers. He was a puppet in the play and nothing more. His team was strong, however, and the group enjoyed some success in spite of him. But eventually his degree from WIIFM (What's In It For Me) University caught up with him and he graduated to the unemployment office along with the other parasites.

Three more self-indulgent scroungers in a business you will never find… and they were all feeding on the Master Lock host at the same time.

The toxic damage done to Master Lock was pervasive. The culture of the business, and the sensibilities of the loyal employees suffered greatly – and it took several years for Master Lock to recover from this psychic assault – not to mention the financial costs stemming from their actions.

Lessons from the days of the parasites

This experience underscored for me the importance of responsible leadership, and the need for disseminating clear and simple values throughout the organization, emphasized and supported from the top down. If management doesn't *Control* or set the values, the group will set their own, and you may not like what you get. Culture can either emerge, or you can shape it – either way it's very powerful, and it will have a dramatic impact on the business over time.

Taking stock

So there you have it. Hopefully the framework provided, along with these examples, will help you construct an inventory of the varied leaders *you* have come across in your life. The really excellent leaders (about 1 in 10) – the vast valley of the Ho-Hum (about 7 in 10) – and the Posers (about 2 in 10).

After constructing your own inventory of leaders – ask yourself what grouping YOU would fall into – and why?

Do others see you in the same light as you see yourself?

Do you take time for introspection to assure that your professional and personal behaviors are consistent with your goals?

Do you lead with positive character, and do you exhibit self-control and resilience as a leader?

Be honest, thorough and courageous in your assessment – beauty marks, warts and all. And ask for candid opinions from others – both your fans *and* your detractors.

Self awareness is critical to long-term success as a leader. "Denial" isn't a river in Africa, and your career can capsize, drowning you in her undertow if you don't heed the rocks, and smartly *Control* your course. As the Roman philosopher Seneca once said, "If one does not know to what port one is sailing, no wind is favorable."

You're the captain...grab the controls

Through my years in business, I've created a model – the *Control + Alt + Delete* model and **The Four Controls of Business Leadership** – that has proven helpful in keeping me on course, and in aiding in the development of my business and personal "peripheral vision." It's a simple guide supporting development of strong and effective leadership. Perhaps it will do the same for you and for those whom you coach and mentor.

THE FOUR CONTROLS OF BUSINESS LEADERSHIP

1. Control yourself – be genuine
2. Control the balance between your head, your heart and your hands
3. Control and value indirect influence
4. Control the balance between your work and your personal life

1. Control yourself – be genuine
- Self awareness is a building block of leadership
- Embrace your strengths and acknowledge your weaknesses
- Lead with your own style – don't be a "book-of-the-month" manager
- Engage your own operating system and define reality
- Be courageous – take appropriate risks and demonstrate resilience when times get tough

35

What does it mean to be genuine? And what's the big deal if you're not? It's just a job, and you can be whoever you want to be at the office, right? Wrong. You will never be an authentic and legitimate leader if you have an air of pretence about you. *Real* people want to work with *other* real people in an honest and open environment.

So how does one go about making sure that his or her behaviors are consistent and genuine – day in and day out? It all starts with recognizing that *you alone* are responsible for your own development.

You...and nobody else.

All too often, I see employees – young and old alike – who opine that their *manager* is responsible for their development – or lack of it. Certainly your manager may provide insights into your capabilities, and *guidance* for your development, but *you* own it. And like most things in life, you usually get out of it what you put into it.

Self awareness is an important building block of leadership, and it is a precursor to self-management. It's about introspection, and taking a full and honest inventory of your strengths *and* weaknesses. This way you can align your behaviors with you goals and values according to your own unique style.

Successful leaders have a broad behavioral repertoire to call upon as needed. These are often referred to as **competencies** (or skills). The trick is to develop your competencies, while maintaining your authenticity... staying true to who you are. You are... where you are today... for a reason. Be a leader of positive character, but do so with your *own style*.

36   Take *Control* of your behaviors by engaging your own

operating system for a couple of minutes every day.

Be realistic, exacting and as fair to yourself as you would be with others. Look at your results – the outcomes of your leadership decisions. Take note of the "wins", and look for patterns that are repeatable.

And even when – *especially* when – you feel your leadership decisions netted a loss – **don't lose the lesson**. Revisit your decisions and behaviors, and recognize the impact those actions may have made on the larger organization. Ask yourself the important question: "What could I have done differently that could have changed or improved the outcome?"

Be in *Control* of yourself and remain genuine, but don't be afraid to take some calculated chances. It's OK to take the road not traveled. Open your arms and mind to change, but don't alter your core values. You can be in *Control* and courageous at the same time if you engage your personal operating system along the way, and use the discipline of the *Control + Alt + Delete* model to guide you.

2. Control the balance between your head, your heart and your hands
  - All three are needed to reach leadership equilibrium
  - Balanced leaders develop healthier organizations
  - Common sense is critical... but not common
  - Form connected relationships with your entire team
  - Be hands-on – learn and teach empirically

Balance. By definition, it means equilibrium and stability. Balance is a state you achieve when two or more parts form a satisfying and harmonious whole, and one element is not out of proportion or unduly emphasized at the expense of the rest.

Effective managers understand the importance of leadership equilibrium, and they work to balance the efforts of their heads, their hearts and their hands. If you are shallow in *any* of these three attributes, you lose your sense of equilibrium, and your effectiveness as a leader will be limited.

Balanced leaders develop healthier organizations, with engaged employees, and an advanced sense of purpose.

Let's start "at the top." The brain is the *Control* center for our nervous systems, governing, among other things, the sensory mechanisms for vision, hearing, taste, smell, touch and equilibrium. It contains over 100 billion neurons, which are the cells that convey information to other cells, managing our bodily processes.

The distinction between the *brain* and the *mind* is fundamental to philosophy. Where the brain is physical gray matter, the mind refers to the stream of consciousness and intellect one develops during life. It's the collective integration of your experiences that translate to and form your beliefs, perceptions, desires, emotions and imagination.

Most leaders have devoted great time and effort to mental development, spending 16+ years in formal schooling challenging their brains, and filling their minds with knowledge. Books and formal classroom instruction allow the "minds of the past" to share their insights and experience to the students of the present. And equally as important are the lessons and insights *you* experience directly and learn first-hand – often the "hard way."

Learning takes time and focus. It can't be delegated. You can't bake twelve-minute brownies in five minutes.

Become an expert in pattern recognition. Examine

different scenarios from your own history and develop axioms of experience. If X… then Y…based on history. This is a great technique to help you evolve your expert intuition. As we grow in life, our minds develop "models" from our experiences and insights. Analysis of past experiences allows us to simulate, or play out future scenarios, and consequently predict outcomes.

Don't undervalue "common sense" – it is simply the digestion and integration of your experiences over time. It gives you context and confidence. It reveals proven truths that you can instinctively rally or default to as needed. And it's the secret weapon of great leaders. Playwright George Bernard Shaw said it succinctly; "Common sense is instinct. Enough of it is genius."

You gotta have heart

To become an excellent leader in the 21st century, it's important that you develop your heart just as fully as your head. This can be a particularly difficult concept to grasp – especially if you are a baby boomer like me.

Boomers were born between 1946 and 1964. We were brought up in a workaholic era where personal recognition and fulfillment had little place in the world of work. Keeping your job and pulling down a steady paycheck were recognition enough for a job well done. But times… they are a changin'. Younger Gen Xers (born between 1965 and 1977) and Gen Yers (born between 1978 and 1994) ask for, need and expect regular feedback and reinforcement. Remember, these younger generations were raised in a world of texting, instant messaging and high-speed internet, giving them instantaneous access to information and ideas.

Employees today expect more than a paycheck and a pension – they seek a sense of purpose. They want open access to their leaders, and they expect them to be forthright. (This is becoming a prerequisite prior to giving themselves *fully* to their jobs.) And they favor interactive learning over the "death by PowerPoint" methods most of us boomers employ.

Consequently, detached leadership doesn't cut it in 21st century business. Emotionally removed leaders will find that they have few followers, and even fewer friends. Leaders must connect with their employees, which takes time, positive energy, focus and often diplomacy. *Learn* the life stories of the people with whom you work. I try to learn at least one new thing about one of my employees every day. (These can be simple things ranging from details about their families... to personal hobbies... to what they did over the weekend.) But however deeply you delve, the connections you form with your team need to be *genuine*. In turn, have the courage, courtesy and candor to let your employees get to know *you* as well. This will help to crystallize their understanding of you, and they will know without question where you stand on important issues

Developing your "qualities of the heart" can be one of the most challenging aspects of growth you'll experience as a leader.

If I were to ask you to choose five words that describe you and your leadership characteristics, I suspect that words like "compassion" and "empathy" would not be at the top of your list. It's important to come to grips with the concept that you can develop compassion as a leader, and still be viewed as strong by your team. They are not mutually exclusive, and in fact, you will be viewed as a more *complete* leader by your organization.

Give your team a hand –

CONTROL +
ALT +
DELETE
Leadership

The concept of "using your hands" in business is about getting in the ring and fighting alongside the rest of your gladiators.

Throughout my career, I've tried to emulate the "hands on" leader style of those I've admired. Testament to that end, I was honored with a plaque from my team at the end of my tenure as President of Canac. (Canac was a multi-national Kohler Company business with over 1,900 employees, and it was the largest frameless kitchen cabinet manufacturer in North America.) The plaque was inscribed with an excerpt from a speech given by Theodore Roosevelt at the Sorbonne (University of Paris) back in 1910. The excerpt has become known simply as "Man in the Arena," and I think it captures succinctly the concept of "hands on" leadership.

MAN IN THE ARENA

"It is not the critic who counts; not the man who points out how the strong man stumbles, or where the doer of deeds could have done them better. The credit belongs to the man who is actually in the arena, whose face is marred by dust and sweat and blood; who strives valiantly; who errs, who comes short again and again, because there is no effort without error and shortcoming; but who does actually strive to do the deeds; who knows great enthusiasms, the great devotions; who spends himself in a worthy cause; who at the best knows in the end the triumph of high achievement, and who at the worst, if he fails, at least fails while daring greatly, so that his place shall never be with those cold and timid souls who neither know victory nor defeat."

Personal experience is critical to learning and growing. I've always found that I can learn a whole lot more away from my desk than I can from sitting behind it. (By the way... you can *teach* a whole lot more away from your desk as well.)

When we retreat to our coveted corner offices, we spend less time "pressing the flesh" out where the action is. Make it a point to *stay involved* with different areas of your business. Roll up your sleeves and get your hands dirty wrestling with the day-to-day problems of your business. Ask questions... learn from others...and share what you know freely with your team.

The Dalai Lama says... "sharing your knowledge is a way to achieve immortality." While it might not deliver *that* lofty a goal, it will certainly make you a more effective leader for the eight-plus hours each day you spend at work!

3. Control and value indirect influence
- Build organization-wide relationships
- Say "please" and "thank you"
- Become an effective communicator

Indirect influence. What is it? Why is it one of the important **Four Controls of Business Leadership**? The aforementioned Doug Dillon and Jim Beardsley both were skilled in the area of indirect influence – in different ways.

Doug used indirect influence to gain support from the sales directors for what became our Top Gun training program. In this case, he solicited "buy in" from his *peers* – individuals over which he had no direct authority. He presented his case, focused on the benefits and persuaded. Winning their support was critical to the success of the program, but what it really did was provide *positive access* to the broader sales organization from which he needed full engagement.

Respected managers (like Kohler's sales directors) help their teams prioritize their actions, acting as "gatekeepers." Their support meant a system-wide investment in the Top Gun program.

As their direct boss, I could have *mandated* support from this group, rather than relying on Doug to win informal buy-in from the team. Had I done that, we never would have achieved the same level of ownership, engagement and support that we ultimately did for the program. With the support of the directors, Doug was able to win over the broader sales team, credibly communicating a shared understanding of the programs importance to them individually, and to the organization as a whole.

Jim Beardsley, despite his "power position" as president and CEO, applied the simple values of courtesy and humility to gain engagement from his employees. He could have mandated, dictated, and generally bull-nosed his strategies and plans – and that's exactly what Ho-Hum leaders and Posers would have done.

Excellent leaders recognize the exponential benefit that comes from having a team of engaged associates working toward a common end.

When associates take ownership of initiatives, they perform their responsibilities because they *want* to support you and the business... not because they *have* to. Excellent leaders recognize this, and empower their employees with responsibility and reward, working laterally and not hierarchically. This includes regularly

employing the "magic words" every three-year-old knows
– "please" and "thank you."

Influence applied to customers, employees and owners

I'm not so naive as to think that there are never times
when the leader needs to be forceful – even a bit
autocratic. It's the job of the CEO to balance the interests
of customers, employees, and the owners of the business –
and sometimes the referee needs to make the call
(*Figure 4*).

In the case of employees, indirect influence can be used
to proselytize them around the interests of customers and

Figure 4:
Balance of
the CEO

business owners. For example, if the CEO is visible getting personally involved in resolving customer concerns – the organization quickly "learns" that customer satisfaction is a business imperative, and they will make it a priority. Indirect influence can prove very effective, and yet it needs to be supported by a vigorous "amen" from the presidential pulpit now and again – hence, the need for regular and candid communication throughout the organization.

In private business, ownership is usually an individual, or a group of individuals. The CEO needs to represent and protect the interests of the owners, and balance it against the best interests of the customers and employees. Again, clear and forthright communication is the means by which to garner support, and indirect influence is your ally.

In the case of publicly traded companies, the importance of indirect influence couldn't be more self-evident. By their very nature, most stockholders are like visiting "tourists". They chose to invest in businesses to make a return – often in the short term. They hang around to catch the sights, grab some earnings, and off to the next site they go.

So business leaders need to be able to present a compelling case to stockholders on why they should stick around a while – maybe even take up permanent residence. They need to influence them to invest in their business, and *stay* invested. Excellent leaders understand this "short-term return mentality" and balance it with the longer-term best interests of the company, its customers, and its employees. They don't succumb to the "damn the torpedoes" 90-day mentality of shallower leaders.

Indirect influence on the "up and up"

In 1985, fresh out of college and armed with a B.S. –
mechanical engineering degree, I began my professional
career with Pella Windows and Doors in Pella, Iowa. At
the time, it was called Rolscreen Company, named for
the company's first product introduced in 1925 (window
screens that rolled up into a metal box at the top of
the window, keeping the screen clean, and offering an
unobstructed view when retracted).

Pella was (and remains) a family-owned company,
with sales in excess of one billion dollars annually, and
employing more than 10,000 associates in North America.
It is the second largest wood window manufacturer in the
United States, and the company enjoys a strong position
in Canada as well. The company was founded by Pete and
Lucille Kuyper, and it has been professionally managed (by
non-family members) for decades.

Pella has a reputation for innovative residential and
commercial windows and doors. Since 1937, the company
has provided consistent industry leadership, focusing
on products with real consumer value, incorporating
the latest advancements in design and fenestration
technology.

My career with Pella began in the role of service engineer.
In two years time, I became well indoctrinated in the
importance of good quality and customer sensitivity in a
company know widely for being one of the best at it. (As
recently as 2007, Pella earned the J.D. Power & Associates
award for "Highest in Customer Satisfaction among
Window and Door Manufacturers.")

After about two years in that capacity, I had the
opportunity to become the product planner for Pella's

residential product line. While the team brought many exciting new products to market over the years, there was one that struggled mightily and taught me an important lesson in how to influence *upward* early in my career.

The president of Pella in the mid-1980's was a man named Wayne Bevis. Wayne had been one of the G.E. "whiz kids", and was among the first in the window and door industry to drive operational effectiveness to unprecedented levels.

Wayne had built a solid team around himself, and he had a mix of tenured industry stalwarts and new talent from outside the industry as his functional heads. Although this mix created an exciting dynamic for the business, it also kept us squarely on the grooved cow path – following the road of the "tried and true" while the new leaders garnered experience and confidence. At that time, ideas that pushed the envelope of innovation were regarded suspiciously at best.

For purposes of background – authentic windows from bygone eras typically had what is known in the industry as "true divided lights." Each window sash had several individual panes of glass that were glazed into muntin bars, creating a series of smaller rectangular patterns, and this allowed for the construction of larger windows without compromising structural integrity (*Figure 5*).

As window designs evolved over the years, the market demanded windows that presented a more "architecturally correct" look than what was available with snap-in muntins (sometimes called grilles), but at a lower cost than that of real divided light windows. Jim Kinghorn, a product engineer and I saw an opportunity to address this need by leveraging some of the new and aggressive temperature- and pressure-sensitive tapes coming on the market from 3M. This enabled

47

us to essentially "slice" a muntin bar in half, and apply the two halves to both sides of a single pane of glass – affixing it permanently – and giving it the absolute visual characteristics of a true divided-light window, at a fraction of the cost.

Figure 5:
Authentic
window
construction

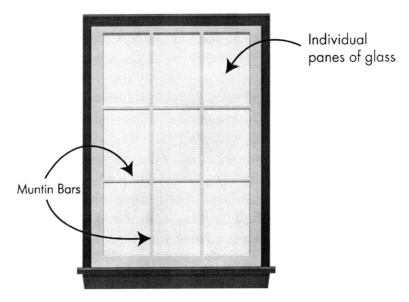

Individual
panes of glass

Muntin Bars

But we were having difficulty getting the attention and support we needed from upper management. Time for a little creative indirect influence!

We created a prototype sash sized to fit one of the windows in the VP of Marketing's office, and installed it on the "QT." We were gambling that when he opened his office drapes in the morning and saw this innovative approach to tradition that we would win his support, and not be issued our walking papers.

The gamble paid off... and we didn't get fired!

Our surprise "show and tell" presentation got his attention, and we were able to influence support to fund and develop the product. (Had we not influenced *upward*, the "Pella Panel Divider" product would have "died on the vine." This product was introduced only in limited production, but it was an important forerunner to what became the highly-successful Architect Series line of windows for Pella.)

So indirect influence is about *pull* as opposed to *push*... and removing the barriers to "yes." Unlike direct authority, which is strictly one dimensional (trickle down), indirect influence is five-dimensional. It works up, down, and across an organization, as well as both inside and outside of the business (*Figure 6*).

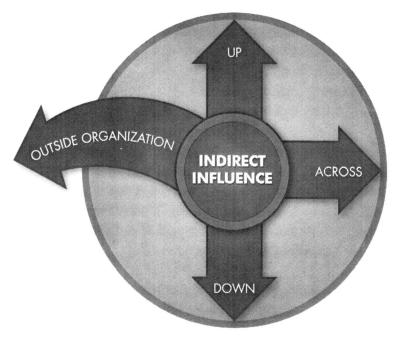

Figure 6: Indirect influence

Often, even when excellent leaders may have the advantage of "absolute authority" they will employ indirect influence for more pervasive – and persuasive – results.

4. Control the balance between your work and your personal life

- Recognize the need and strive for work/life balance
- Your career is a marathon – not a fifty-yard dash
- Leave a legacy – what do you want it to be?

Work/life balance. Is it a dichotomy? Is it an unachievable contradiction? Can professional success and a satisfying personal life ever truly be reconciled? Well, today's employees not only *believe* it, they're *demanding* it.

A recent Hudson survey of 1,634 workers who have been in their current jobs for at least five years, ranked the primary reason that they accepted their current positions. The top responses:

Work/life balance and flexibility	29%
Compensation	23%
Work culture	13%
Training opportunities	5%
Advancement opportunities	5%

Are you surprised by these results? Maybe – maybe not. The work/life balance challenge has weighed heavily on executive brows for decades, but never has it been more difficult to achieve than in present times. We all want it – and yet it's usually the last aspect of our lives that gets needed attention and energy.

The "Protestant work ethic" on which most of us were raised never considered such a thing. Consequently, most of us still offer our families, significant others, and ourselves only whatever's left over at the end of the day – far less than what they truly deserve. We get engrossed chasing dimes, and we lose sight of the real treasure. We become hypnotized by work and the prospect of success. We multiply our assets, and compromise our ideals along

the way. We end up living to work rather than working to
live. We accept a humdrum existence and lose touch with
ourselves and those closest to us when we should be
adding verve to our lives and depth to our relationships.

But there is an extraordinary and satisfying sense of
totality that comes from a more balanced approach.
Broadening your exploration now can have a profound
and positive impact on both your professional and
personal life. There isn't a "rewind button" on life, and we
can't go back in time later to add back the experiences we
should be enjoying to enrich our lives today.

Don't be just a human *being*, become a human *doing*

Relationships for 21st century professionals have become
particularly tricky to balance. Not because they are overly
complicated to build and nurture, but because we move
those relationships to the back burner of the stove while
we're cooking up our careers.

We don't want to miss out on the slightest opportunity to
"get ahead." Competition is keen, so we limit our quality
time with our significant others, cancel and shorten
our vacations, and justify our way into a more stoic and
mundane life – by choice! What's more, the profusion
of electronic communication "conveniences" keeps us
tethered to work like never before – practically around
the clock.

A loving, supportive home is your due. Treat your career
more like a marathon than a fifty-yard dash, and mind the
pace accordingly. There is nothing more fulfilling
than sharing the joys and sorrows of life at an intimate
level with your partner. Remember what brought you

together in the first place, and don't let your relationship erode over time. Don't take your relationship for granted – take it to the next level.

Decades of medical and scientific advancements have extended the average life expectancy in the United States to 77 years (80 if you happen to live in Canada). A company pension or a 401K is "cold comfort" at the end of your day and the end of your working life.

Get started now. Approach your personal life with the same focus and enthusiasm that you bring to the office, and recognize that just as businesses change and evolve, so do people and relationships– often in different ways and at different paces. Monitor your relationships just as you would your business, and communicate regularly. *Control* its development. *Alt* course corrections as needed. And *Delete* the things that can derail you from your life goals.

Celebrate fully – often – and simply

- Hold hands often and appreciate the tender moments. (Don't keep your affection bottled up like a genie in a magic lamp. Uncork the lamp often and let your affection out so your partner knows that he or she remains paramount in your life.)
- Surprise her on a Saturday morning and treat her to breakfast in bed. Take him to a baseball game or sporting event that you know he likes.
- Have a candlelight dinner together under the stars on a beach with your toes in the water, or just stick a couple of tiki torches in the ground by a table in your backyard and create a new world.

- Take her out to dinner and have the restaurant place a single long-stemmed red rose on her plate before taking your seats.

- Visit an amusement park and ride a few roller coasters together.

- Yuk it up together at a comedy club on a weeknight.

- Challenge each other mentally, and also recognize the importance of silly fun nonsensical stuff (See if you can figure out together why some flamingos are pink, and others are white. Have fun discussing whether or not wheat germ is something transmitted by sickly wheat. Find out whether or not you think the hokey pokey really IS what it's all about!).

- And when you're at work, carve out a few moments to send your significant other an instant message, email, or text...just to let him know that you're thinking of him. Use these electronic tools that tend to take *away* from your relationship to help you *build* upon it as well.

Build your life and your legacy

As I've spent most of my professional life in the home building products industry, I thought it might be apropos to leave this section with a short parable about a carpenter to think about as you look to build on your life and your legacy. Consider this:

An elderly carpenter was nearing the end of his career and wanting to enter retirement. He approached his employer and shared with his boss his plans to leave the home-building business and live a more leisurely life with his wife, and enjoy time with his extended family. He would certainly miss the paycheck, but he felt he needed to retire.

53

The employer was sorry to see his good carpenter go, and he asked if he would be willing to build just one more house as a personal favor. The carpenter said "yes," and he began to work on the new home. In time, it was easy to see that the carpenter's heart was not in his work. He resorted to shoddy workmanship and he used inferior materials in this home. It was an unfortunate way for him to end a dedicated career.

When the carpenter finished his work, the employer came by to inspect the house. Upon meeting the carpenter at the front door, he handed the carpenter the keys. "This is your house," the employer said to the carpenter. "This is my parting gift to you."

The carpenter was grateful and shocked. What a shame, he thought. If only he had known he was building this house for himself, he would have done it all so differently. He wouldn't have used inferior materials, and he would have provided a higher degree of quality workmanship.

And so it is with us. We build our lives, a day at a time, often putting less than our best labor and materials into the building. Then with a shock, we realize we have to live in the house that we've built. If we could do it all over again, we'd do it much differently, but we can't go back. Remember... there's no rewind button on life.

You are the carpenter. Each and every day, you're placing a board, hammering a nail, or erecting a wall. Your life is one big DIY (Do it Yourself) project. Your choices and actions that you make today build the house you'll live in tomorrow. Approach this construction project with a plan, and build it wisely.

SECTION 1 IN SUMMARY

We opened this section introducing you to the "keys of organization" – the *"Control + Alt + Delete"* model. This simple model gives you the daily *structure* you need to keep your professional and personal development on goal.

We discussed three different types of leaders (excellent, ho-hum and posers) and defined the characteristics of each. We profiled the good, the bad and the ugly... and discussed the importance of responsible leadership in business.

And we closed out Section 1 with a detailed discussion of **The Four Controls of Business Leadership.** These *Controls* can be used to help guide your development as an excellent leader of character – well suited for the challenges of business and life in the 21st century.

SECTION 2
Managed Change

Managed change is all about putting the *"Alt"* and *"Delete"* keys to work for you. We don't live in a simple black and white world; most of our lives are spent living in varying shades of gray. Consequently, in both business and in your personal life, there is often more than one right answer. More than one path you can choose to achieve the desired result. Which begs the question… does the path you choose to get there really matter? Does the end justify the means? I believe that how you get there does matter… a great deal… and leaders of character recognize the importance of choosing proper path. Your "Alt" and "Delete" keys can help you chart the passage, allowing your clarity and positive character to define you in the end.

Fundamentally, both the *Alt* and *Delete* keys on your computer keyboard are modifier keys. They help you *manage change* while doing work on your computer. *Alt* is used to change the function of another key. For example, if you press the letter "H" on your keyboard, it will type the letter "H." If you depress the *Alt* key along with the H key, your computer will perform an *Alt*-H function. (On my computer, it pulls up the "help" menu). The *Alt* key can also be used in conjunction with other keys, like the tab key, to switch between windows. Or, it can be used to

57

access pull-down menus… which give you options. The *Delete* key is all about command editing and discarding unwanted content. Plain and simple.

Although *Alt* and *Delete* are both modifier keys, they play very different roles on your computer keyboard. And, together, they symbolize two powerful "strokes" that help you to evaluate – and emulate – excellent leaders of character.

Managed change

Managed change. It sounds easy, doesn't it? And yet dealing with the twists and turns of fate during the circuitous daily course can be more daunting than one might expect. Why? Because we are creatures of habit by nature, and we build up *inertia* against change as we carry out our daily lives. Like the flywheel on a farm tractor, we gather energy and resist changes, releasing pulses of energy as needed to stave off attempts at altering our speed or our course.

Change is hard. Change can be painful. Ask anyone who's tried to quit smoking or drinking. Ask a marriage counselor or divorce attorney about a couple's plans to "change" the other. Hard… and painful… and sometimes impossible… or inappropriate.

Inertia is a very powerful force – both positive and negative. It's one of the principles of classical physics that we all studied back in high school. As Sir Isaac Newton taught us… *Bodies in motion tend to stay in motion. Bodies at rest tend to stay at rest.*

58

"Iceberg...right ahead!"

Sometimes attempting to institute change can make you feel like you're trying to change the course of a large seagoing vessel. There you are on the bridge, at the captain's helm, actively turning the wheel, but it takes a long time before the bow of the ship begins to move in the direction intended.

Picture in your mind's eye *The RMS Titanic* – steaming across the North Atlantic under a dark evening sky on her maiden voyage from Southampton, England to New York City, when the two lookouts on duty spotted a large iceberg directly ahead of the ship. They sounded the ship's bell three times and telephoned the bridge exclaiming, "Iceberg, right ahead!" First Officer Murdoch ordered an abrupt turn to port and full speed astern, which began the process of stopping and reversing the ship's engines.

The ship's forward inertia was too strong to overcome in short order, and the ship could not turn to the port side fast enough to avoid the devastating collision. The ship struck the iceberg on her starboard side, buckling the hull and allowing water to enter between her steel plates, eventually succumbing to the onrush of water, until she reached her final resting place on the floor of the Atlantic Ocean.

The logic... of "dominant logic"

A specific form of *business* inertia I'd like to discuss with you now is that of "dominant logic." C. K. Prahalad and Richard A. Bettis are credited with first introducing the concept of dominant logic back in 1986. In summary,

59

their suggestion is that top managers in a business deal
with increasing requirements for strategic decisions,
(often caused by acquisitions or structural changes), based
on their cognitive orientation (or biases). It's the prevailing
wisdom *within* you – about how the world works *around*
you – and how you need to interact *within* it.

Said another way... there is an old axiom that says
"experience is the best teacher." While both history and
experience are certainly irreplaceable professors in our
lives, learned behaviors or "dominant logic" can be both
blinding and restricting if they go unrecognized.

Don't think that you're susceptible? Let's look at a couple
of simplistic exercises that might help you better relate to
this concept as it plays out in business.

Try this.
Stand up, and allow your arms to rest comfortably at
your sides.
Cross your arms in front of you.
Take note of which arm you laid on top of the other.

Drop your arms back down again comfortably at
your sides.
This time, cross your arms in front of you, but put the
opposite arm on top.

It feels quite different, and in most cases... unnatural,
doesn't it? And yet you've still accomplished the act of
crossing your arms.

Or:
Reach down and untie both of your shoes.
Now tie the shoe on your right foot the way you always do.
Then try to tie your left shoe the *opposite* way.

Most people will tie their shoes using a simple bow knot. It's created by forming two half knots – one on top of the other. Depending on how you learned to tie your shoes, you will either draw the left loop over the right loop, or the other way around.

Doing a familiar task in a new way not only feels weird, it doesn't come easily. And unless you consciously work at engaging differently, you will automatically, instinctively revert to habit.

Well, just like individuals, businesses and organizations exhibit "dominant logic." And that's not all bad. For one thing, it's safe, familiar, and proven. It helps lay out how an organization has been successful in the past, and it often defines the parameters of its operations. The existing "dominant logic" can help to reduce ambiguity, and provide a framework to help sort out complex issues and choices. These are its merits.

But beware its drawbacks!

Dominant logic is linear, and it centers on accepted views and processes. If it's used myopically, it discourages different views and it can preclude healthy diversification. In fact, it becomes an easy and safe default position or a "crutch" for the business when faced with change. After all… it's the established way.

People and businesses don't, by their nature, reevaluate their logical approach every time new information is received. In fact, they use their dominant logic to interpret the new data and its meaning. If dominant logic in a business is rooted in sound principles and its managers apply it with flexibility, it can help enable the company to leverage and build upon its strengths and steadily and consistently grow. It can take what could be a stumbling block, and turn it into a stepping stone.

Successful companies are those that recognize that throwing down anchor in the safe harbor of "dominant logic" can constrain a business model, and keep it from sailing into opportunistic waters. Over time, companies that don't recognize this become more and more entrenched in their current models, and they miss opportunities that could offer significant growth and success.

"Game changers" of modern civilization

Let's ferret this out a bit and look at a handful of specific inventions that challenged dominant logic, and impacted human civilization in a profound way... taking us way beyond the status quo.

1. The light bulb. Thomas Edison challenged the need to turn to oil and wax for evening illumination. He not only developed the first viable incandescent electric light (in 1879), but created the electric lighting infrastructure required to make the incandescent light practical, safe, and economical. In 1882, the first commercial power station was activated in lower Manhattan, providing light and electric power to customers in a one square mile part of the city. In 1889, Edison General Electric was formed. (Interestingly, Thomas Edison never controlled the company, even though it included his name.) As the industry grew, Edison General Electric merged with its leading competitor – Thompson-Houston in 1892. At that time,

Edison was dropped from the name, and the company simply became known as... General Electric.

Edison's challenge of dominant logic brought us cost-effective light and electric power... hence the practice of "burning the midnight oil" could be carried out by us workaholic executives with the simple flip of a switch instead of the flicker of a lamp!

2. The telephone. In 1876, Alexander Graham Bell said "goodbye" to dominant logic when he said "hello" to Mr. Watson... "come here – I want to see you" (and some teenagers haven't been off the phone since!) Up until then, the predominant communications vehicle was the "wireless" telegraph. One need only look around at  the ubiquitous use of cell phones to understand the impact of this revolution. They're in every car, on every street corner, in every line at the deli, and in the seat behind me at every movie I try to enjoy! Mr. Bell's invention has allowed people to speak instantaneously, and over long distances, bringing people closer together around the world.

3. The Model T automobile. Henry Ford challenged dominant logic on two fronts: transportation by beast and production by batch! He began producing "cars for the masses" in Michigan around 1913–14. The Model T was first introduced in 1908, but cars didn't become popular until he was able to mass produce them on an improved assembly line, making the product affordable. A Model T could be assembled in just 93 minutes, changing both mass production and mass transportation forever. Manufacturing of every stripe benefitted from the cost-controlled organization of the assembly line, and Americans enjoyed a new-found freedom that came with affordable car ownership.

4. The jet engine. Sir Frank Whittle and Dr. Hans von Ohain winged away from dominant logic and propellers as co-inventors of the jet engine. They worked independently, and each knew nothing of the other's work. Mr. Whittle was the first to register a patent for the turbojet engine in 1930. Hans von Ohain was granted his patent for his own turbojet engine in 1936. Hans von Ohain's jet was the first to fly in 1939, and Frank Whittle's jet first flew in 1941. The jet engine remains the workhorse of the world's airline industry today, and without question, has made the world a much smaller place, bringing people of different countries and cultures physically together in mere hours.

5. TV dinners. "Dinners are to be cooked in the kitchen and eaten at the dinner table." So said dominant logic until Gerry Thomas invented the Swanson TV dinner in 1954. It combined the attraction of saving time with society's new-found fascination with the television. Early TV dinners cost $.98, and they featured such staples as meatloaf, Salisbury steak, turkey and fried chicken. Rounding out the dinner was a small helping of potatoes, a vegetable, and later... desserts. Over 10 million TV dinners were sold during the first year of national distribution alone. "Fast food" of all kinds followed suit, and Americans have been "eating on the run" ever since.

6. The microwave oven. As with many inventions, the microwave oven was actually the by-product of another technology. Around 1946, Dr. Percy Spencer, an engineer with Raytheon Corporation, was testing a new vacuum tube called a magnetron, when he noticed that the candy bar in his pocket had melted. Intrigued by this, he tried some additional

experiments. He placed some popcorn next to the tube – then an egg. The popcorn popped, and so did the egg! In 1947, the first "Radarange" was put on public display. They eventually evolved from commercial use to the countertop models used in residential homes, challenging the dominant logic of cooking over fire or in a pan. By 1975, sales of microwave ovens exceeded that of gas ranges.

Flush with innovation – A deep plunge into the creation of The Kohler Hatbox toilet

A more recent example of recognizing dominant logic and challenging convention in new product development is Kohler's Purist Hatbox toilet.

Kohler Company was founded by John Michael Kohler in 1873, and has been under the leadership of Herbert V. Kohler Jr. (a grandson of the founder) since 1972. Under Herb's leadership, Kohler Company has grown to become one of the largest privately-held business concerns in the United States. It has done this through consistent execution of its business models to gain competitive advantage and leverage and through excelling in new product development.

The dominant logic of the company, as played out in the area of new product development, is significant and entrenched. It provides the architecture by which new product opportunities are identified and developed. (Most companies have a product development process that they follow for new product development, but Kohler's, I dare say, is one of the best.) They take a robust approach to "mapping" out new product ideas, and managing those ideas from concept to commercialization.

They start with the creation of a five-year "new product schedule," reviewed by senior management twice each year. Then, as products are being developed, they are subjected to a "design review" process, wherein the "crispness" of the design is examined, making sure that the physical aspects of the products are spot on. Costs, pricing, market positioning and launch plans are also reviewed to optimize the chances of success in the marketplace.

This is where the premise of *Control + Alt + Delete* comes in.

If adjustments are required to either the products or their positioning, the *Alt* function is invoked and changes are managed – right then and there. If they are not on strategy and it's determined that they can't get there – they're *Deleted* – also right then and there. No further questions asked, and no additional time wasted trying to justify or "bail out" a misdirected effort.

66

Crown vitality king

New product vitality is king at Kohler. New product development is resourced, managed, and measured. Kohler tracks new product sales using what is called a "vitality index." It's an indication of portfolio vitality, or "freshness."

Rubbermaid is credited with creating the vitality index measurement years ago, and it's a means by which to measure the degree to which your business is remaining dynamic, and to keep offerings from becoming stale.

The specific vitality index measure varies with different companies, but basically it involves measuring the percentage of sales from products that have been introduced over a specified period of time – generally between one and five years. Some consumer products companies and technology companies use a shorter measurement period, while durable goods companies tend to measure to a longer timeframe. Kohler uses a three-year measurement window.

Most durable goods companies would be pleased with a three-year vitality index of around 20–25 percent, meaning that 20–25 percent of their sales revenue within a given year would be from products that were introduced within the previous three years. Consumer products companies aspire to drive vitality rates in the 30–50 percent range – depending on the product category.

It's in the DNA

Kohler is a durable goods company – yet in categories like plumbing, it consistently delivers higher vitality results more reflective of a consumer products company. That's by design...not by accident. Their commitment to new product vitality is embedded in the very DNA of the business, and it's supported by the "dominant logic" of its leadership. That consistent focus, sustained over time, has netted Kohler a significant industry leadership position, from which it builds inertia, leverage and subsequently market share.

Intelligent, well placed "dominant logic" is hardly static. Kohler's openness to new product ideas has become part of its very successful bedrock and this consistent commitment to new products and innovation has well served both the company and its discriminating consumers.

Numbers tell the story

Kohler is not alone in this regard. Other companies like 3M, DuPont, Johnson and Johnson and Rubbermaid, to name a few, understand the heightened sales and profits a company can enjoy by earning a new product leadership position.

The Product Development and Management Association (PDMA) performed a detailed study of 416 practitioners at North American companies across industries in 2004. Companies in the top third of their respective industries enjoy *more than double* the amount of sales and profits through vitality products (as a percentage of their total sales) than the rest of the competitors in their industries.

New Product Sales as a Percent of Total Sales, 2004

	Top 1/3 of Industry	Rest of Industry
Sales from New Products	46.1%	21.4%
Profits from New Products	49.1%	21.2%

• *source: PDMA 2004*

So we understand the importance of innovation management – and we may even be able to spark such a culture in our operations. But how does one *maintain it* such that it is absorbed and reproduced in a business' "dominant logic" over the long haul? After all, there is a constant "tug of war" going on between the left-brain (creativity) and right-brain (logic) camps within the business. Success, then, requires the creation of a level playing field – one that promotes healthy balance between the two.

In a fight between a bear and an alligator – the outcome is determined by the terrain. Although both are powerful animals, you can likely project the winner based on whether the fight is staged on land or in the water.

Similarly, successful organizations balance the corporate terrain such that neither the right nor left brain aspects are advantaged – resulting in either the stifling of innovation, or the flooding of "newness" at the expense of crisp execution. Let's examine the delineation of the business brain functions:

Left-brain	Right-brain
Creativity	Discipline
Culture	Processes
Tacit knowledge	Explicit knowledge
Innovation	Productivity/efficiency

These are all necessary abilities, and when properly fused and harnessed can help a business become a real product development powerhouse!

Create and design with passion. Then implement with science. Reinforce a culture that opposes imitation and the ubiquitous lack of influence it creates over time.

Continually press the team for innovation that is meaningful to the *consumer*... not just product line extensions with "feature creep." (Don't accept new features creeping in... for *features* sake.) Make certain that the *benefits* derived are meaningful to your customers so they will continue to vote for you at the cash register.

Time pressure can impede creativity, and great discipline is critical during this phase or you may get stuck in the R&D "spin cycle" – resulting in the product either never being brought to market or in "spinning up" costs at an alarming rate.

You need room for exploration and risk when developing new technology...and you need acceptance of failures. Take it from one of the great "explorers" of our time – Thomas Edison. No doubt, he achieved greatness with his many inventions... but he also had countless misses along the way. In his words, "I have not failed. I've just found 10,000 ways that won't work."

Perfect ideas usually aren't floating around the R&D lab like feathers in a pillow factory, and they don't always materialize the first time out. In fact, first ideas are often "kludges." A kludge is a clumsy or inelegant solution to a problem, produced in a well-intended attempt to satisfy a consumer need. Yet each small failure contributes to the development of breakthrough products, so take the time up front to get the basic architecture right - then *Alt,* or make iterations as needed to assure that the end product is on strategy.

Bio of David Kohler – a champion of change leading the way

David Kohler is President and COO of Kohler Company, and he's one of the three children of Herbert V. Kohler Jr., and great grandson to the company founder.

David is a gifted and resourceful leader who grew up in the business. He received his Bachelor's Degree in political science from Duke University in 1988, and he worked in various manufacturing jobs at Kohler during his summer vacations while attending high school and college. Upon graduating college, he became a foreman in the cast iron division – then left in 1990 to earn a Master's Degree in marketing from the Kellogg Graduate School of Management at Northwestern University. Following a year with Dayton Hudson, he returned to Kohler as director of fixtures marketing for the plumbing business.

After a successful stint in leading the marketing team, David was promoted to vice president of sales for plumbing – then sector vice president and general manager of Plumbing North America. In 1997, he became sector president, and he was elected group president for the kitchen and bath group in 1999, joining Kohler Co.'s board of directors that same year.

I've enjoyed working with David through the years, and we grew to become both business associates and friends. His hallmarks include a refined ability to think, reason, and understand. He has a sharp strategic mind, strong intellect and executive balance, and he's willing to challenge convention.

But that's not what sets him apart as a unique and excellent leader.

David is a more complete leader because of his qualities of the heart. He has an uncommonly engaging approachability and genuineness. (As the son of an industry icon, one can imagine how difficult it must be for him to maintain his individuality – rather than just trying to emulate the behaviors of his successful father.)

David has a lovely wife, three young children at home, and another in college. He shares his life stories with co-workers, and he makes himself accessible to listen to theirs. He's a confident leader and confident leaders ask for help all the time. He's not concerned about being viewed as less than "all knowing." He's demonstrated the courage to allow people to have a sense of who he *really* is, and that insight allows the team to know where David sits on important issues. It inspires the team to get behind his leadership and ideas, which are the derivatives of his intellect.

How about a little toilet talk?

And now let's "talk dirty" about an invention that isn't often the topic of conversation in "polite society" – but without which society would be a whole lot less "polite" – **the toilet**. (Let's start with just a wee bit of history, and perhaps some biased perspective on my part.)

No other invention has accommodated the size and con-centration of civilized populations more. Without the toilet (and it's supporting waste treatment infrastructure) high-density cities would not be possible (or certainly not pleasant). Tossing the contents of chamber pots into the streets and waterways is literally "medieval" and ultimately fatal.

Advanced ancient civilizations, like the Greeks and Romans, created systems that provided running water to their citizens. The Roman aqueducts were engineering marvels for their time, bringing fresh water to cities across southern Europe. Yet even these civilizations had yet to devise a consistent method for removing waste from individual residences. Latrines were communal. Public "co-ed" areas with rows of bench seats were positioned over running water, and "guests" used sticks with a sponge at the end for self-cleaning.

By the early 1800's, the pollution and unsanitary conditions in Europe and America required the ingenuity to improve upon what the ancients did centuries earlier: draw clean water into the cities, and remove waste to bodies of water outside of the settlements. In the 1800's, iron foundries and potteries developed and perfected terra cotta pipe for underground sewage systems – the first critical passage in making the outhouse obsolete.

By the late 1800's, "wash-out" toilets of various designs were being developed simultaneously in England and America. In fact, a "wash down" toilet design is commonly used throughout Europe to this day. Here, water is driven through the rim of the toilet, and it "washes down" the inside of the bowl to remove the waste.

In America, the siphon jet toilet is the accepted standard. Sanitary manufacturers discovered that if you diverted some of the water from the cistern to the bottom of the bowl, it creates a "siphon jet" action which helps to remove the waste.

Given the way this invention revolutionized and literally "civilized" the modern world, it is impressive that it is, at base, a very simple concept. What's more, given the technological advancements in toilets themselves, and the increasingly "green" emphasis on their efficient use of water, the fixture has remained relatively unchanged for more than a century. Much like even the most primitive of "privies," today's standard toilets have a bowl, a tank acting as a water reservoir above and behind the bowl, a seat and a lid.

So when you look beyond the new colors and style enhancements of any toilet of today, you're really looking at hundreds of years of dominant logic. The toilet is… what it is… because conventional wisdom and *dominant logic* says that's what they should look like, and how they should perform.

This "dominant toilet logic," began to meet some challenges in 2003/04 when Kohler began developing new pieces for a plumbing suite called "Purist." These products follow a very clean, streamlined, minimalist-inspired aesthetic (*Figure 7*). During the development of the Purist Hatbox toilet, David Kohler took a personal interest in challenging convention. He exhibited leadership balance by taking a "hands-on" approach and getting directly involved with the development team from the very inception.

As this product began its journey through their new product development process, David offered a bold challenge to the team: to disregard the prevailing wisdom and functional cues of the traditional toilet, and develop a product with both exceptional flushing performance, and a strikingly simple design. (New ideas pressing the limits of established convention like this weren't exactly getting tossed around like horseshoes at the company picnic!)

*Figure 7:
Kohler's
Purist suite*

This ran counter to the organization's dominant logic that had built a successful plumbing fixtures company on the "traditional" and "time tested" design concept. But David's personal involvement was critical to providing that "level playing field" so necessary to give the concept more than just a fighting chance. He supported the industrial designers in their passionate quest to push the design envelope, and coordinated with engineering to assure the right amount of science was baked into the design for great performance. "Right brain" and "left brain" were balanced.

Key to this product was its 0.2 horsepower electric pump. The Power Lite™ pump technology had been used by Kohler for some time in more traditional toilet designs for commercial applications, requiring consistently-high flushing performance. In the case of the Hatbox, it allowed the designers to develop a "tankless" product, stressing the geometry, clarity and precision of the minimalist design school.

An electronic "soft touch" actuator was placed on the side of the toilet, and the water supply lines could be routed through the floor, hidden from view, leaving an almost furniture-like fixture that's visually simple yet striking. (You may have guessed by now that the resulting product had the visual cues of a large hatbox... hence the toilet took the name "Hatbox."

Figures 8 & 9: Kohler's Purist Hatbox toilet

In 2005, David Kohler said, "By rethinking the toilet with no preconceptions, Kohler has laid the groundwork for the next generation of toilets. The Purist Hatbox toilet project challenged Kohler design associates to combine bold innovation, enhanced technology and great design to create a product that has redefined how we perceive the toilet." Now this very product is challenging the established dominant logic of the design community, freeing them to place the Hatbox where toilets have never been placed before. Out in the open – not hidden from view.

Design curator and owner of Luminaire®, Nasir Kassamali, said, "Kohler has completely rethought the design of a toilet. By internalizing all of the requirements for functionality, the exterior has become a simple, well-proportioned container. This toilet can be incorporated anywhere in the modern bathroom."

Now that we had an unconventional toilet in the Hatbox, We needed an unconventional, high-profile platform from which to introduce the product to the world. Dominant logic would call for introduction at one of the two large industry trade shows that we participated in annually: the International Builder's Show (IBS) or the Kitchen and Bath Industry Show (KBIS).

Again, David pushed the team to challenge accepted convention and the trade show "dominant logic." The venue he supported instead was New York City's Fashion Week (February, 2005).

Fashion Week takes place twice each year in New York City's Bryant Park. This eight-acre space gets transformed into a temporary fashion arena with temperature-controlled chalets complete with elevated runways, mood lighting, high-energy music, and models sporting the clothing collections of the world's top fashion designers. (Designers range from Oscar de la Renta to Zac Posen, and guests include A-list journalists, buyers, celebrities, and elite fashion-centric consumers.) This progressive, high-design and eclectic group provided the perfect audience to launch the new Purist Hatbox toilet to broad acclaim.

The Hatbox exhibition area told our story and demonstrated the product to Fashion Week guests and the press. Additionally, Kohler supported the event with mobile executive bathrooms featuring Hatbox toilets, so participants had the opportunity to experience the product first-hand. (You can imagine the starkly appreciative reaction this received over the plastic "port-a-potties" that traditionally serve as "powder rooms" at these functions.)

This is just one simplistic example of how dominant logic was recognized and challenged, resulting in positive press, category prowess, expanded name recognition, and increased market share.

The "bottom line" on the Hatbox

The "bottom line" on the Hatbox? Well, it remains to be seen what hidden potential was unlocked by breaking from established patterns of design and what form that will take among future products. But of greater significance is the lasting impact on the *organization* that came from challenging the established cultural norms and decoupling the unconscious constraints around creative thinking. So it's not so much *what* was created... but *how*.

Kohler took the time needed for exploration. Some clumsy executions appeared, out of the gate, and accepted as part of the process. Ultimately they got the architecture right, and they *Alt*ed many iterations along the way to assure the Hatbox was on strategy with *real consumer value – not "feature creep."* Credit David Kohler with recognizing dominant logic, and supporting this effort with openness, advancing design well beyond today's status quo.

Controllable and uncontrollable change

Often, change can be managed at one's own discretion; individuals and organizations can manage change on a voluntary basis. You may choose to *Alt* some important lifestyle changes, such as smoking, exercising, or making sure you spend quality time with your significant others. Or you may choose to *Alt* changes around your professional life, such as forming connected relationships with your co-workers, or going back to school to expand your academic knowledge.

Businesses also make *discretionary changes* that can be self-managed. (These changes can be affected toward the strategy, structure or culture of the business.) A *strategic* change may be deploying resources toward a new sales channel, or entering an entirely new business segment. *Structural* changes might include undertaking business reorganization, or launching a broad-based CRM (Customer Relationship Management) program. *Cultural* changes are the most difficult to manage, and they tend to be less tangible. (These may include behavioral and policy changes to more fully align the organization with its core values.)

Regardless of the scenario, the point is that we all make *Alt*s and *Delete*s to our courses on a *voluntary* basis, and we do our best to manage the timing of those adjustments so we can execute those changes in an effective and organized manner.

The more difficult change management challenges are the ones that we don't have fundamental control over, and these can be remarkably disruptive to our lives and businesses. Scholar Reinhold Niebuhr said it well; "God, grant me the serenity to accept the things I cannot change, the courage to change the things I can, and the wisdom to know the difference." These changes outside of our control are the significant events that tend to cause stress in our personal lives, and challenge the capabilities of our organizations.

Getting personal

In 1967, two psychiatrists, Richard Rahe and Thomas Holmes, examined the medical records of over 5,000 medical patients to determine if there was a relationship between stressful events and illnesses. Forty-three "life events" were characterized and scored on a relative basis.

Interestingly, we often tend to think of stress as being linked exclusively to "bad" things like death, divorce, or losing your job. But, just as often, "good" events can add to your stress level as well – things like marriage, retirement, or having a baby.

The Holmes and Rahe research has been published as the Social Readjustment Rating Scale (SRRS), and is also referred to as the Holmes and Rahe Stress Scale. Below is a summary of the forty-three life events and their relative scores, in descending order, from most to least significant. (The higher the score, the more stress you are likely to experience when subjected to that particular life event.)

Life Event	Life Change Units
Death of a spouse	100
Divorce	73
Marital separation	65
Imprisonment	63
Death of a close family member	63
Personal injury or illness	53
Marriage	50
Dismissal from work	47
Marital reconciliation	45
Retirement	45
Change in health of family member	44
Pregnancy	40
Sexual difficulties	39
Gain a new family member	39

Business readjustment	39
Change in financial state	38
Change in frequency of arguments	35
Major mortgage	32
Foreclosure of mortgage or loan	30
Change in responsibilities at work	29
Child leaving home	29
Trouble with in-laws	29
Outstanding personal achievement	28
Spouse starts or stops work	26
Begin or end school	26
Change in living conditions	25
Revision of personal habits	24
Trouble with boss	23
Change in working hrs. or conditions	20
Change in residence	20
Change in schools	20
Change in recreation	19
Change in church activities	19
Change in social activities	18
Minor mortgage or loan	17
Change in sleeping habits	16
Change in number of family reunions	15
Change in eating habits	15
Vacation	13
Christmas	12
Minor violation of law	11

According to this scale, the total number of "Life Change Units" (adding together the scores for all events that occurred in one year of a person's life) indicates the degree to which stress may affect your health. Here's what the bandwidths look like:

Score of 300 +: At risk of illness
Score of 150–299: Moderate risk of illness (reduced by 30 percent lower than the above)
Score of 150 –: Only a slight risk of illness due to stress

Calculate your own relative stress level. If you're running on the high end of the bandwidth, recognize that you are dealing with stress levels that could significantly affect your health. Invoke your personal operating system, and distinguish between those factors on the list that you can and can't *Control*. Then take inventory; assess what really matters, and use your *Alt* and *Delete* keys to help you find balance. Institute any changes you can to reduce your stress level, and seek professional counsel for guidance and assistance as needed.

Stress and opportunities to manage change are critical to the health and growth of organizations and businesses as well. Here are just a few examples of significant events that can create "shock" and significantly stress a business, and the people functioning within it:

Financial crisis
Ownership change
Merger or Acquisition
Going public
New leadership
Loss of leadership

Leadership in crisis – the Plymouth Foam story

Managing change through stressful times is never more critical than in times of crisis, and an organization for which I've served as a Board of Directors member was faced with one of the most significant "shocks" that a business can possibly face – the instant and simultaneous loss of the entire top leadership tier of the company.

Plymouth Foam, headquartered in Plymouth, Wisconsin, was founded in 1978 by Tecwyn ("Tec") Roberts. It began as a regional supplier of expanded polystyrene products (EPS), and remains a family owned business today. Plymouth Foam has grown to become one of the nation's leading manufacturers of rigid and soft foam products, with multiple production facilities located throughout the Midwest.

The company serves a diverse group of commercial and industrial customers from three business divisions. The Building Materials division manufactures building and construction insulation products for both residential and commercial construction. The Protective Packaging division supplies businesses with custom-designed and mass-manufactured protective packaging materials. The Custom Solutions division manufactures products for a diverse group of customers, and often their foam products are incorporated into others on an OEM (original equipment manufacturer) basis.

The company also makes products for the garage door industry, and insulation products for both interior and exterior wall applications. Additionally, Plymouth Foam products are used in roofing applications, and as lightweight fill for road and bridge construction, as well as in the construction of retaining walls and foundations of buildings.

Biographies of a family leadership team

Tec is an engineer, and he successfully managed Plymouth Foam well into the late 1990's, when he transitioned the ownership and management of the business to two of his sons. Vance Roberts, Tec's eldest son, was Vice President of Development and Technical Services. His expertise was process development, and he was also responsible for managing the creation and introduction of new products for the company.

Vance's younger brother Scott became President and CEO of the company. Together, they worked to expand upon the solid business foundation that their father built, and to position Plymouth Foam for a prosperous, thriving future.

Scott and Vance both had technical backgrounds by education, and they were both professional engineers. Scott also obtained an executive MBA from the University of Wisconsin – Milwaukee. They worked together with good chemistry, and both took a hands-on approach to the business.

While Scott and Vance managed the business, Tec created a working board of directors to help guide the development and growth of the company, which took shape in late 1998 and early 1999. Tec, Scott and Vance were active on the new board, and they went outside the business to recruit other successful business people with diverse skill sets to help shape strategy.

All A-board

The quality of the board Plymouth Foam was able to assemble was quite remarkable – considering the size of the company. It was comprised of accomplished businesspeople of excellent character, and its chairman was Tom Testwuide, Sr.

Tom received his Economics degree from Marquette University, and he worked for A.O. Smith Corporation before joining Schreier Malting Company in 1971, ultimately becoming its Chairman, President, and CEO.

In 1994, the company received the prestigious Wisconsin Manufacturer of the Year Grand award, which is a testament to his leadership. (In 1998, Tom sold Schreier Malting and its subsidiaries to Cargill, Inc.) Today, Tom is active on several industry, bank and charitable boards in addition to providing steady leadership as Chairman of the Board and CEO at Plymouth Foam.

Another powerhouse pick was John Viglietti. John received his BA degree from Lake Forest College and an MBA from the University of Chicago. He spent the early part of his career with Fansteel Metal Corporation, and Simpson Electric.

John was integral to the growth and success of American Orthodontics, where he worked from 1970 until his retirement in 2002. As president of American Orthodontics, John was a pragmatic and well-balanced leader, who added dramatically to both the top and bottom lines of the company. Under his leadership, annual sales of that company grew by a remarkable 330 fold! Chances are that if you have a child wearing braces today, many of the products in your child's mouth, and the tools in the hands of your orthodontist, came from John's company.

What's more, the respectful working environment created by John is evidenced by the fact that American Ortho consistently had employee turnover rates of less than one percent during his tenure.

The third outside director was Tom Lopina. Tom is an accomplished financial executive and a deeply principled businessman. He was CFO for Ariens Company, and he was also president of Gravely, a commercial power equipment company in North Carolina. Most recently, he was owner of Spectrum Solutions management consulting company in Oshkosh, Wisconsin. Tom's level demeanor and sincerity serve him well, and people around him quickly become comfortable working with him, knowing that he's the genuine article.

In 2002, Scott Roberts invited me to join the board as the fourth outside director. As the management team began to focus on growth, he felt that I might be able to help add value in the areas of marketing, sales, and business development. I was flattered by the invitation, and excited to have a chance to both work with, and learn from, the talented group that Plymouth Foam had assembled.

The board gelled nicely in the months and years that followed as we created and executed Plymouth Foam's strategic plan.

Acuity of focus

The strategic plan for Plymouth Foam focused on three distinct areas: growth, efficiency, and personnel development.

Growth was deemed important for the company to gain scale and offer leverage in the market – to generate greater profitability from higher asset utilization. The leadership team developed strategies to support better organic growth, and the organizational structure was adjusted for better customer and market responsiveness.

(Plymouth Foam sequenced the correct way. *Strategy* should **ALWAYS** come before *structure*. All too often, businesses and organizations skip the important strategy part, and they just climb onto the reorganization merry go round instead. Up and down...

around and around... adding churn and confusion to the business, and no real value to the company or its customers.)

Reorganizations need to have a purpose, and this raison d'être should ultimately deliver improvements in either efficiency or effectiveness or quality of product – if not all three. Having an effective organizational structure is important, but having a crisp, executable strategy that's understood by all those in the business MUST come first.

The balance of POWER

It takes both *knowledge* power and *position* power in the same room to work strategic issues effectively.

As the board and the management team began setting strategy, we were careful to *include* the voices of those from Plymouth Foam with the best perspective of the market, our customers, and the competition. This included the business management team, and also some key mid-level managers. (This is very important under "normal" business conditions, and it becomes mission critical when a business is distressed.)

I've been involved in three significant business turnarounds in my career; two were successfully righted, and one was not. I've witnessed first-hand the calamity that develops when you "corporatize" or centralize the setting of strategy, i.e. when those with *position* power exclude those with *knowledge* power, and strategies void of their important insights are created. In this particular case, we assembled monthly with the highest levels of corporate management to discuss the issues of the distressed business. And although this business was

87

ancillary and quite different than the core business with which our senior executives were more familiar, we quickly limited the *knowledge* power in the room. (Read that to mean we overpowered the operating business participants with corporate executives in these meetings by a ratio of 5:1. To work strategic issues effectively, the ratio should be almost 1:1.)

For perspective, I was involved with this distressed business for two and a half years, and I could count on less than my two hands – the number of times any of the corporate position power brokers – the ones who were setting strategy – either visited one of the manufacturing plants, or visited with a customer. The power brokers tipped the balance, and the resulting strategies were out-of-touch and ineffectual. It also created an atmosphere of division and alienation – the last thing needed while trying to save a flailing enterprise.

Check your egos at the door

Chief executives have the *position* power, but in most instances, lack the real *knowledge* power they had as members of the rank and file. Our egos might suggest otherwise, but the fact of the matter is – the higher up one moves within an organization, the further removed he or she becomes from the pulse of the day-to-day business. Not because we *wish* to be, but rather because of the other managerial and administrative tasks that tugs on the coattails of our time.

Executives should certainly establish objectives for the business, but those with the *knowledge* power should develop the strategies and tactics to deliver those goals. Then, all members must be accountable. Responsibility *and* authority need to be in the hands of the business team.

Lessons from *successful* turnarounds

A successful business turnaround must be strong and balanced in two key areas to be successful – strategy and finance. Visionary leadership, and the ability to cascade that vision effectively throughout the organization is extremely critical. Without that communication, associates don't understand WHY change is necessary, much less their role in the success of the company going forward.

If a company is going to survive – much less thrive – all associates must have a high level of understanding and engagement. Set the strategy, and stick to it. If you continually change the strategy, you will create even deeper confusion and chaos in the business, and your employees and customers will disengage. Been there – done that.

Once your strategy is 85–90 percent complete you can begin to focus on execution. (If you wait for the "perfect strategy" to fall out of the sky, land on your face and start to wiggle – you're going to be waiting a long time!)

In addition to clear strategy, it's important to have strong financial leadership. Strategy helps provide insights into what you can *Control* as a business, and it should also define those aspects of the current environment that you *cannot* control. Then finance becomes the *Alt*, or modifier key, to guide execution.

Most of the time in business, access to resources (people

and cash) is a zero-sum game, meaning that if you are going to deploy them to support activity in one area of the business you have to take them away from someplace else. There usually isn't a pool of additional associates, or bags of extra cash lying around to aid you in fixing the business... no secret glass "rescue vault" in the CEO's office that says "break and use in business emergency."

Its simple math, but the decisions around redirecting resources can often be painful, and that's why clear understanding of strategy is so important. And it's also why you need strong financial leadership to provide balance. Together, this will give a clear understanding of your costs, and an accurate inventory of both your business and human capital.

In challenging times, you need a financial leader who is *proactive* - not just a passive meteorologist. A strong and proactive financial leader can help you get to where you need to go much more quickly and solidly. Make sure you have that strong financial leadership entrenched in your organization, and use it to help *Alt* the business as needed.

So the four key steps in the recipe to a successful turnaround?

Set the strategy – communicate it broadly – stick to it – and focus on execution.

Structure FOLLOWS strategy

In the case of Plymouth Foam, "divisions" were created to help the team better deliver on the customer promises outlined in the strategic plan. We *Alted* resources away from lesser-valued pursuits and focused them behind more meaningful products and services (as valued by the customers) to keep our existing base and attract new business.

In today's knowledge-based economy, having fewer, better people will help move a business along proficiently, and we found and empowered two excellent leaders in Mike Borzcik and David Bolland. Mike Borzcik as vice president of Manufacturing, and David Bolland as vice president of Sales and Marketing.

Mike Borzcik was a skilled engineer and experienced in manufacturing management. He received his BS in Industrial Engineering from the University of Arizona, and an MS in Business Management from American Technological University. He was an Engineer Officer with the 62nd Engineering Battalion in the U.S. Army, before a distinguished career with International Paper. He joined Plymouth Foam in late 1999, and became vice president of manufacturing in late 2001. He brought process improvement to the operations through the introduction of new disciplines in measurements and quality – always with an eye on "safety first."

Dave Bolland was a young, yet accomplished marketing executive when hired in 2003. His degree in business administration was from the University of Wisconsin, and his MBA from the University of Arizona. He had a clear track record of results, with prior stints at PepsiCo, and Bemis Manufacturing Company. He had good listening skills, demonstrated willingness to direct change, and exhibited the characteristics of an excellent leader.

Dave learned the business by asking good questions of both our customers and employees. He brought a level of sophistication that was lacking in the marketing/business development area, and was largely responsible for aligning the "front end" of the business around market segments as opposed to geography (as had been the mildly effective practice in the past.)

Mike Borzcik and his operations team was charged with driving efficiency improvements, and Dave Bolland and his team were focused on profitable growth.

The third leg on the strategy stool for Plymouth Foam was personnel development.

Talent search

One of the most important responsibilities of a board of directors is to understand the capabilities of the team, and assure that internal talent exists to provide orderly business succession.

This is not as easy as it sounds. Leadership can take on many forms, and it can be difficult to quantify and qualify. A good track record in the past isn't always money in the bank going forward. Can you distinguish between a good manager and a good outcome?

Just because you made it safely down river doesn't mean that you're an expert navigator. Sometimes the currents of strong market conditions, favorable currency exchange rates, competitor blunders, or just plain luck can carry a company "safely down river" – skewing reality. Similarly, even the raft with an excellent helmsman can be cast upon the rocks due to unforeseen eddies, such as legislated or environmental restrictions, unfavorable currency rates, or other macro-matters outside of his or her control.

standards, ship on time, and pursue new markets and new customers."

Both Scott and Vance's widows subsequently joined the board, and we welcomed their involvement and fresh insights. They proved clear in communicating their wishes, and confident that a capable and experienced professional management team was in place to help the business with the "heavy lifting."

Could your business survive a shock like this?

Fortunately for Plymouth Foam, we had a meaningful succession plan in place, the workforce and management capabilities to survive a shock of this magnitude. Ultimately, Plymouth Foam went on to have its most profitable year in the history of the company in 2006 – testament to the adaptive capacity of the business, its leadership, and its collective ability to *Alt* managed change.

One important lesson from the Plymouth Foam story is the importance of risk management – and that includes assuring capable leadership is in place to carry a business forward. Even in the face of the seemingly unimaginable.

If you're not familiar with how to get started in succession planning, you'll find a host of information available to you on the web. Below are two simple resources to get you started.

Dale Carnegie offers a white paper entitled "The nuts and bolts of succession planning." This simple and thought-provoking piece was written by William Rothwell, and you can access it through dalecarnegie.com. You can also get good, free information on succession planning from the website of the Small Business Administration at **www.sba.gov.**

Smart companies plan for the future. A Hewitt Associates study done in 2005 showed that of the top 20 leadership-oriented companies in the U.S., nearly all of them (95 percent) have a CEO succession plan in place. This compares with less than 60 percent of other companies. Similarly, 85 percent of these same top 20 companies have an emergency succession plan, while only 59 percent of other companies do. If you don't have a succession plan in place for your business, the time to do so is now.

Experts in this field suggest the following:
- Succession planning is a process, not a singular event
- Identify potential successors and include them in the planning process
- Begin by assessing your company's current state
- Create objectives that reflect the values and culture of your company
- Establish a timeline and cadence around succession planning
- Create meaningful development plans to grow the capabilities of your team.

SECTION 2 IN SUMMARY

We opened this section talking about the importance of managed change, and the impact that inertia can have – both positive and negative.

We discussed dominant logic as a type of inertia, and the importance of acknowledging it, enabling businesses and their individuals to move beyond the unconscious boundaries it unknowingly establishes.

We explored the Purist Hatbox toilet as an example of the value that can be created by challenging accepted convention.

We discussed stress and the importance of managing change with *Alt* and *Delete*.

And we closed out this section with the story of Plymouth Foam, and how this remarkable company was able to withstand what could have been the crippling loss of its leadership team. It's a compelling story about adaptive capacity, highlighting the responsibility of senior management to assure that a solid business succession plan is in place.

Used smartly, the *Control + Alt + Delete* leadership model can help you navigate successfully through the expected – and recover from the unexpected.

SECTION 3
The Quest for Work/Life Balance

"I like nonsense, it wakes up the brain cells. Fantasy is a necessary ingredient in living, it's a way to looking at life thru the wrong end of a telescope. Which is what I do, and that enables you to laugh at life's realities." – Dr. Seuss

How I wish I had come across this astute "Seussian" quotation earlier in my life. In his own idiosyncratic way, he hints at the need for perspective and balance in one's life – something I've struggled with personally – as have most of my contemporaries.

I learned about the importance of having proper work/ life balance and clear communication with loved ones the hard way. As I cruised along the river of professional accomplishment, I left a turbulent wake of failed marriages behind me. Three...to be exact. My drive for success took on a very high priority, and it came at the expense of work/ life balance and my marital relationships.

I've endured the heartaches and headaches that result when you don't integrate all aspects of your life into a harmonious whole, causing your loved ones to look outside the marriage to find the "missing pieces." Even good people   **99** make bad decisions from time-to-time, and poor communication and improper work/life balance fosters an environment where even *Miss Guided* can become *misguided.*

In divorce, pain is inevitable... but self-pity and suffering are optional. As the noted sociologist Oliver C. Wilson says – *"What poison is to food, self-pity is to life."* I've worked hard to learn from my own shortcomings, so I can use that knowledge to benefit my current relationships. It's said that a smart man learns from his mistakes, but a truly wise man learns from the mistakes of others. I'm hoping *my* experience will similarly help *you.*

... I'm assuming, by the way, that your work/life scale is off balance and, what's more, that it's the "life" side of the scale that needs the weight added to get you back on center. I say this based on years of observation and experience. If, however, I'm being presumptuous and your scale is unduly weighted in the *life* direction, you can put down this book at this point... and start calling the TV talk shows and the tabloids. I'm sure they'd LOVE to profile you! For the rest, read on.

First – is it even possible? Is work/life balance just another impossible contradiction in terms... a dichotomy or oxymoron like honest politicians, military intelligence, airline food, jumbo shrimp, fun run and death benefits???

I'm going to try and assure you that it is, with the support of: disciplined time management, proper priorities, and clear communications. Hopefully what I've learned will help some of you avoid the absolute *worst* of fictitious dichotomies... "friendly divorce!"

But it's going to require real effort and, quite possibly, a revised perspective and a new course as you navigate the

uneven currents of contemporary culture that are
flowing against you.

Many societies have established and ingrained into the
human psyche that there is an important distinction
between "work" and "life" or "leisure." This sociological
"norm" took root in the late 18th and early 19th
centuries. Sweeping change in the entire western world
– in manufacturing, agriculture and transportation –
markedly created and reshaped the "cultural landscape."
This pivotal point in history (often referred to as "the
Industrial Revolution") fostered the stark demarcations
of "work" as our primary purpose, and "leisure"
as a frivolous, unimportant (if not interfering and
undermining) "sideline."

This antiquated, one-dimensional, destructive view is a
bit like Grandpa Abe Simpson (the fictional character
from the animated TV series "The Simpsons") shaking a
curmudgeonly fist at the sky and screaming, "The metric
system is the tool of the devil."

And in the 21st century, the situation is even more
complex and challenging.

We now live in a global economy, which has us
competing not only with Peter in the cubicle to our left,
but also with hoards of faceless, nameless professionals in
far-flung China and India.

As businesses become increasingly multi-national, video
conferences, web networking and phone calls extend our
mornings and evenings to all time zones and all times of
the day (and night). The workday never ends…

Plus technology makes the marketplace truly ubiquitous,
24/7. Wi-fi capable laptops, Blackberries and cell phones

go with us everywhere, transforming our homes, cars and vacation resort hotel rooms into virtual extensions of our offices.

Family structure has changed, too, with dual-career couples, single parents, and expanded commitments to our loved ones, friends and communities.

I want to be crystal clear in stating that I'm not an apologist for hard work. Quite the contrary. Work is good and necessary. It challenges our minds, pays our bills, and offers personal fulfillment as we contribute in a positive way to society. Our contemporary work ethic, however, bolstered by modern technology, has created a dramatic collision of priorities in our lives, and it's left many of us feeling disjointed, incomplete and/or dispirited. We've forgotten how and when to raise the "yield sign" and grant our personal lives the "right of way."

If you neglect your family, you'll likely miss out on what are truly once-in-a-lifetime events, like your child's school play, your parent's anniversary, or your wife's high school reunion. These opportunities are fleeting. Missing the important milestones will take its toll over time, eroding – or failing to construct – critical family history and "connectedness."

Trusted friends are also an important support group that should not be taken for granted. If you don't nurture those friendships, you may find yourself at a loss when the chips are down and you need them most. Just as importantly, you'll miss out on a lot of love and laughter and good times!

And let's not forget about your physical health. If you overwork and become fatigued, your professional life can suffer along with your personal life. When you're tired, your ability to think and your hand-eye coordination is reduced. This makes you less productive, and more error – and possibly injury-prone.

Like the links of a chain, our personal lives and professional lives are intertwined and connected. And much like a chain, if any one link weakens and fails, the integrity of the *entire* chain is compromised, leading to personal discord and/or poor work performance... possibly even putting your career in jeopardy. And yet when all the links are holding fast and true, the chain works as intended, and you can pull through anything in your life.

A healthy personal life should be the bedrock upon which everything else is built, and this is why work/life balance is so important. Your relationships bind everything else in your life together, and a loving atmosphere at home can prop you up and allow you to breathe when the world inevitably kicks you in the sternum and would otherwise knock the wind out of you.

Remember...work is about what you *do*. Leisure or life... is about who you *are*.

The first two sections of this book focused on the professional side of life, and how **The Four Controls of Business Leadership** can help you recognize – and become – an excellent leader of character in the workplace. Now we'll apply the same principles and tenets to the personal realm.

To be clear – Dr. Phil I'm not. Nor do I pretend to be. Developing and growing meaningful relationships is a mix of both science and art. If it's science you seek, there are plenty of psychology books and science journals written by gifted doctors and psychologists in the library and on the web to address your needs. The focus here is on the "art" and some practical ideas from some of my experiences, to help you avoid the hazards that can "break your chain," and dispatch your relationship to Dysfunction Junction.

So often we find ourselves totally spent by the time we get home at the end of the workday, and our significant others "get" from us what little is left over, rather than what they truly deserve. We either don't communicate at all, or we do so with an "irritable edge" because we're tired, or we don't want to be challenged. We've multi-tasked at a maddening pace all day long... and then we continue the onslaught by bringing the marketplace home with us, tethered through technology. The line between our professional and personal lives has been erased, and we unwittingly alienate our loved ones, and fracture the relationships that matter most.

Striking a smart work/life balance in this increasingly competitive and fast-paced world we live in is no simple undertaking. Difficult... yes... but it's not Copperfield magic either. You have the ability to take *Control* of your work/life balance, and reduce the level of stress both you *and* your loved ones experience when things are off kilter. This simple two-part strategy may help you strike a healthier balance:

Part 1: Time Management and Setting Priorities

Part 2: Expressive Communication

Time Management starts with fully understanding how you spend your day. Once you have made a reasonable assessment, you can protect what is "value added" and worthwhile, and target time wasters and unnecessary activities. This can be done through one of two techniques.

First: *Save* **time by eliminating, combining or delegating activities, opening up time that you can use for something else.**

Some simple examples: *Eliminate* the 15 minutes you spend each morning making a special trip for a cup of coffee. Make one at home instead. *Combining* tasks might mean running all errands during one outing rather than making several trips to stores on an ad-hoc basis. *Delegating* might include outsourcing things like house cleaning and cutting the grass to a trusted neighbor kid.

Second: *Invest* **time in something that will save you time later.**

A simple example might be to take a typing class. (If you spend as much time on the computer as I do, it's amazing how much more you can get done – and in far less time – if you're skilled on the keyboard.)

Setting Priorities involves controlling what you can, and invoking your *Alt* and *Delete* keys to remove the "non-value-added" aspects of your day. This will enable you to put your time and energy into what matters most.

Expressive Communication means going beyond the superficial and expressing yourself fully and honestly through "thought, word and deed" with your loved ones. It's also about recognizing the power of the *"non-verbal"* in your household and in your life.

Part 1. Time Management and Setting Priorities

Time management in and of itself can be a complex and time-consuming topic. Some people will devote days sitting through seminars, trying to learn the latest techniques... usually leaving with a fat three-ring binder of rhetoric that ends up on an office shelf gathering dust.

But in the interest of time management, I'm going to show you a simple tool that you can grasp in about five minutes, and put into practice immediately. The tool is called the "Eisenhower Matrix." (Sometimes referred to as the "Eisenhower Method," or the "Time Leadership Matrix.")

As its name implies, it is a method said to have been used by Dwight D. Eisenhower, and summed up in a quote attributed to him: *"What is important is seldom urgent and what is urgent is seldom important."* The way I look at it... if this simple model was good enough for the 34th President of the United States to help him run the complexities of an entire country (not to mention successfully commanding the allied forces in WWII)... by God, it ought to be a good enough tool to help us manage the challenges of *our* days! (*Figure 10*)

The matrix is divided into four quadrants. The vertical scale is a measure of a task's relative importance (the y axis), and the horizontal scale is a measure of a tasks urgency (the x axis). To make this easy to follow, I've numbered the four quadrants for you, and I've put a smile, frown, neutral face, or a garbage can on the matrix to help you visually discern where you want to spend your time.

The Importance Scale: If an activity is important to you, it gets a smiley face. If it's not important to you, it gets a frown.

The Urgency Scale: If the activity is urgent, it gets a frown, as it requires priority attention whether you want to provide it or not. If it's not urgent, it gets a smiley face, because you can take on the activity at a less pressing pace.

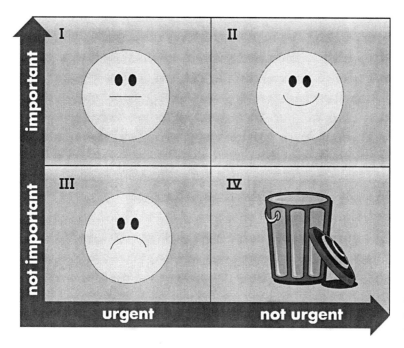

Figure 10:
Eisenhower
matrix

Quadrant 1: These are activities that are important to you, and carry a high sense of urgency. These activities get a neutral face, because they are important to you, yet you have to do them at a rapid pace.

Quadrant 2: This is your happy place. These are activities that are important to you, and they have a lower sense of urgency or time pressure. That means you can tend to them when you want to, and with minimal stress.

Quadrant 3: These activities get a frown. They are minimally important to you, but need to be done with a sense of urgency. (Usually, that means they are important to *somebody else.*)

107

Quadrant 4: This is the waste quadrant. It captures activities that have minimal importance to you, and little or no time pressure associated with accomplishing them. (Ergo, the garbage pail icon.)

Using this tool is really quite simple. To begin, record everything that you do for one week in a rudimentary log. Keep track of both work-related and non-work-related activities. Then sort through the activities and decide which ones are necessary, and the degree of importance they carry for you. Then consider the relative urgency with which these activities need to be carried out, and plot them on the matrix.

Visually "speaking," this is our objective:

The goal is to maximize your activities in Quadrant 2. These are the activities that are important to you, and they have limited time pressure (read that to mean lower stress).

- Tasks in Quadrant 4 (the waste quadrant) are simply eliminated. Time can then be redeployed for activities in Quadrant 2.

- Tasks in Quadrant 1 are *important* to you *and urgent.* These are usually done personally by you.

- Tasks in Quadrant 3 should be delegated or assigned to someone else (if possible) as they carry a lower level of importance to you… (yet they may be considered urgent by someone else).

- Tasks in Quadrant 2 (your happy place) are typically undertaken by you, and you can schedule them into your day by *planning ahead* since they have lower urgency.

As you look to expand Quadrant 2, here are some suggestions:

1. Understand your options. Does your employer offer flex hours? Can you compress your work week, or work from home occasionally to reduce time spent commuting?

2. Batch the thatch. Organize your household tasks. Combine errands to minimize drive time. Do a load or two of laundry during the week so it doesn't become an overwhelming chore on your day off.

3. Just say "NO." Get comfortable with the idea that it's OK to respectfully decline some requests – both at work and in your personal life. Once you have a handle on what your Quadrant 2 looks like (your happy place), don't flood your day with activities that are in your other quadrants. When you quit taking on activities out of guilt or a false sense of obligation, you'll free up time for the activities that are truly important to you.

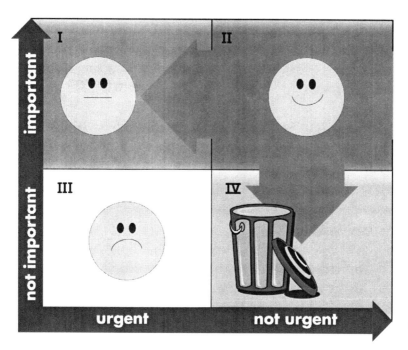

Figure 11:
Eisenhower
matrix goal

4. Don't forget the neighbor kid. If you can afford it, look to outsource activities that carry lower importance for you. Let him or her rake the leaves, cut the grass, clean the house or wash the car. You need the time, the kid needs the cash, and you'll probably make a new friend in the process.

5. Be just a little bit selfish. Make time in your day for an activity that you alone enjoy... and that you enjoy *alone*. Take a walk, work out at the gym, read a book, laugh at an episode of Family Guy, or take a relaxing bubble bath. Do it... guilt free. Nurture yourself and it will help you deal with the rest of your otherwise hectic day.

6. Avoid panic at the disco. Keep a visible weekly/monthly family calendar of important dates and activities to avoid last-minute surprises and panic.

7. Week night – rec night. Try and set aside one evening each week for recreation... even if it's only a couple of hours one evening a week. Turn off the TV, leave the cell phones on the kitchen counter, and discover new activities you can do with your partner, family and friends. This will rejuvenate your spirit, and enhance your important relationships.

8. Sleep tight and don't let the bedbugs bite. Make sure you get enough sleep during the week. If you're sleep deprived, your productivity is reduced, and you are more prone to make errors. This could cause you to work even *more* hours... get even *less* sleep... and perpetuate the vicious cycle.

9. On the seventh day... God rested. *You* should, too. Pick a day off and protect it. Move other activities and routine chores to the other days of the week so you can enjoy the *complete* relaxation of this day off.

Whether you choose to use the Eisenhower Matrix in a *formal* sense or not, hopefully you find the concept easy enough to grasp that you can *save* and *invest* time and energy more wisely, opening up room for your more important Quadrant 2 activities. Activities that are important... but not urgent. Activities that you can schedule smartly into your day, reducing stress and increasing your personal satisfaction.

Part 2. Expressive Communication

Almost everything pertaining to the health of a relationship and achieving healthy work/life balance begins and ends with communication. I doubt this comes as a major newsflash to most of you. And yet most of us don't dedicate proper time, energy and *thought* to it, and certainly not on a regular, daily basis. Employing good communication skills are like any other kind of workout – these "muscles" must be consistently exercised to grow and become strong and healthy.

Communication is so much more than spoken words. Sure, what we say is important, but in relationships, the nonverbal behaviors... what we *do* as opposed to what we *say*... are the "acid test" of our sincerity and commitment.

Consider this. Albert Mehrabian, Professor Emeritus of Psychology at UCLA, has become widely known in psychology circles for his publications on the relative importance of verbal vs. nonverbal communication. In his studies, Mehrabian comes to two key conclusions. First, that there are three elements in any face-to-face communication:
- Words (seven percent)
- Tone of voice (38 percent)
- Body language (55 percent)

(*Note* – this became known as the "7%-38%-55% rule")   **111**

And secondly, that the *nonverbal* elements are particularly important for communicating *feelings* and *attitude*. Let's face it – that's what communication in relationships is all about – expressing your feelings and attitudes. And although verbal output can be turned off, nonverbal cannot. Even silence communicates something... and sometimes silence is the best course!

It's important to be aware of the power of the nonverbal message. In fact, in a head-to-head between the verbal and nonverbal, the nonverbal will win the communications competition every time. *Telling* your significant other "I love you" carries some meaning. But *showing* your significant other "I love you" trumps the spoken word handily.

That said, I've created a model to help add heft to the "life" side of your work/life balance scale – "**The Executive's Guide to Expressive Communication.**" (These "action items" are disproportionately biased toward the nonverbal for the reasons cited.)

The Executive's Guide to Expressive Communication

Communicate Day and Night
Offer Mulligans
Manners Matter
Make Time
Unexpected Little Things
Nibble and Hold Hands
Inclusion
Call Daily
Annual Living Sprees
Tech Respect
Emoticon

♦ Communicate Day and Night

"I am quite sure that no friendship yields its true pleasure and nobility of nature without frequent communication, sympathy and service."

George E. Woodberry – author and poet

There is nothing more fulfilling than sharing life's intimate joys and sorrows with your partner. And yet, as simple as it sounds, most of us struggle to do it. This usually happens because our personal lives take the back burner of the stove while we are cooking up our careers. We treat our careers more like a 50-yard dash than a marathon, and the pounding pace of chasing business success becomes numbing to our feet, our heads, and our personal relationships. Then when things go south with our loved ones… we wring our hands, scratch our heads and wonder what happened to that "jump from the riverbank – first-time feeling."

We compound this negligence daily, and the "law of diminishing returns" is entrenched before we know it. And that's a tough rut to climb out of. Inertia works against us… and that ol' Industrial Revolution dominant logic tells us "that's OK."

Instead, approach your personal life with the same vigor that you bring to the office, and recognize that just as businesses change and evolve, so do people and relationships.

Communicate in a clear and respectful manner with your significant other – both day and night – and build upon the things that brought you together in the first place.

Pillow talk is especially healthy and highly recommended.

Perhaps it's because the setting or atmosphere is less threatening or confrontational... or that we are not absorbed in the duties of the day. Either way, we become "softer" at night... more intuitive and open. It's a welcome time to connect with your partner and become "tuned in" to what annoys or impresses him or her. It's an environment that fosters understanding and helps keep the relationship even.

◆ **Offer Mulligans**
"Forgiveness is an act of the will, and the will can function regardless of the temperature of the heart."
Corrie ten Boom – Holocaust survivor

If you've ever played golf, I'm sure you know what a mulligan is. For you non-golfers, a mulligan is a free "do over" that one golfer grants to another after an errant shot... usually after driving the golf ball out of play. Like "gimme" putts, they are prohibited in the official rules of the game, but quite commonplace in *social* golf.

The origin of the Mulligan

There is considerable debate about the origin of the term. According to the United States Golf Association (USGA) there are several clubs and many individuals who have laid claim to its spawn.

The story most widely accepted focuses on a gentleman named David Mulligan who played at the St. Lambert Country Club in Montreal, Canada during the 1920's.

Mr. Mulligan was an hotelier in the early 1900's. He was part-owner and manager of the Biltmore Hotel in New York City, as well as several large Canadian hotels. One

114

day, as the story goes, Mr. Mulligan hit a very long drive off the first tee... but sliced the ball out of bounds. Acting on impulse, he re-teed another ball and hit again. His playing partners found this flagrant liberty quite amusing. Mulligan himself called it a "correction shot," but his playing partners quickly coined the shot a "mulligan." Here endeth the golf history lesson for the day!

The Game of life

Like golf (unless you're Phil Mickelson or Annika Sorenstam) life is one big *social* game, isn't it? So grant and ask for mulligans in your relationships. And forgiveness is crucial to "fair play" so don't be like a buzzard picking at the bones of yesterday's faults and failings. In disagreements with your loved ones, deal with the *present*... not the *past*.

When you open up a quarrel between the present and the past, it's the *future* that you sacrifice.

Granting mulligans can be difficult to do, and some people struggle more with "letting things go" than others. One of my ex-wives admittedly was one who struggled in that regard. Whenever we got into wrestling with current issues, she would reach back and pick at scabs of three, four, and five years prior. She held in scorn and acrimony like a fish stick holds in heat after being pulled from the oven... and it charred our relationship.

It takes time for walls to crumble, but it's important that you tear them down like an old abandoned house... or the walls can become jail cells... imprisoning the future with the past standing a watchful guard. Spend your energy communicating, in a respectful manner, with eyes forward – that's where the serenity is. Learn to "let go." Be the first to grant your significant other mulligans or "correction shots," and just like in social golf, your partner just may reciprocate.

♦ Manners Matter

"The great majority of successful business men and women have been and are possessors of strong personalities of the right sort, and by analyzing their climb to success it is amazing to discover how large a part good manners, good breeding, and correct behavior have had in helping them to win the goal."

Ida White Parker – author

You understand the importance of good manners and professional etiquette in business, or you wouldn't be enjoying the level of success that you do. Manners are the staples of civilized culture; they telegraph meaningfully and credibly the respect and reverence you hold for others. As a leader, this is critical as it facilitates candid business dialogue, making associates feel more comfortable and less vulnerable to attack or belittlement.

But why are so many of us quick to forego proper manners at home? I'm not talking about eating with our mouths closed, or keeping our elbows off the table... legitimate as they might be. I'm talking about manners reflecting *courtesy* and involving *charm* – the kind of things that were important during the courting phase of your partnership. Some of these may be "standard fare" and others may be unique to you.

Drag them out of the mothballs and try them on again. You may be surprised how well they still "fit" and shocked by how attractive they make you to your partner.

And it doesn't have to be a big production number – just using "please" and "thank you" regularly is a great place to start. Earlier I mentioned Jim Beardsley, and how his use of proper manners and etiquette established a corporate-wide culture of respect at Master Lock. Jim was just as respectful and courteous to his wife Peggy, both publicly and privately. It was an inspiration to witness and no doubt helps account for the Beardsleys' long-standing marriage.

Some suggestions for the gentlemen:
- Regularly open her car door.
- Hold an umbrella over her head to keep her dry in the rain.
- Walk down the stairs ahead of her, and up the stairs behind her. (This ritual started so that the man can "catch" the woman if she trips or falls.)
- When you're walking down the sidewalk together, keep her farthest from the street. This way she is more distant from the traffic, and shielded from anything that might spray up as oncoming vehicles pass by. (This custom has roots in the old west when "traffic" was mostly wildlife and the roads were plenty dusty or muddy!)
- When dining out at a nice restaurant, stand whenever she leaves the table. (Some gentlemen will also stand on her return, but this could be a little "over the top.")
- Let her sample the wine, and wait for her to take the first bite of her entrée before taking yours.
- Don't begin to eat at home until she is seated, and insist that the children do likewise.
- If she prepared dinner, thank her for it. Every time.

Some suggestions for the ladies:
- Have a sympathetic ear. Showing interest in his immediate concerns is complimentary.
- Control "talkativeness." By nature, women have a

stronger drive to speak than men. Allow him his time and turn.

- Use good table manners and social conduct. "Europeanized" manners are attractive to the contemporary man. In the words of famed British author Henry James, "The torch of tradition, a little more neglected by each generation, burns dim and smoky."
- Protect and time honor the pleasantries, charm, manners and good taste prevalent in European countries – and help resuscitate them in the Americas.

Display *visible signs of genuine respect* for your significant other, expressed through your *actions*. It will help you form good habits for admirable living, and set the foundation for open and meaningful communication at *home*. And in *public*, use your PDA a lot... and I'm not talking about your "Personal Digital Assistant," but rather "Public Displays of Affection!

♦ **Make Time**
"Patience and time do more than strength or passion."
    Jean de La Fontaine – 17th century French poet

This, to me, says something about *reflecting* before *reacting*.

It also speaks to the emotional sustenance of treating every day as a special occasion and virtually "eating off your good china." (Contrast that mindset against the force-fed, dine-and-dash, drive-thru, paper-plate lifestyles and attitudes by which most of us have conditioned ourselves to live today.)

It says something about "the gift of time" being of greater

worth when you wear your Timex watches and mark time

together... instead of "investing" in higher-priced Rolexes and nothing else.

And it says something about the therapeutic aspects of quieting your mind, daydreaming, and just plain *thinking* without the disturbances of multi-tasking or the bombardment of media. (It's ironic that when we see someone "just gazing out the window" we brand that time as "wasted." It's OK to put down your pencil, turn off your phone, and just plain *think* for a while. Enrich yourself and allow your brain to "stretch" a little each day so as not to get mushy in the mud of the mundane tasks.)

♦ **Unexpected Little Things**
"My creed is that: Happiness is the only good. The place to be happy is here. The time to be happy is now. The way to be happy is to make others so."
Robert G. Ingersoll – politician and orator

A surprise 40th birthday party. An anniversary dinner at a swanky restaurant. These are valid recognition marking *significant* events. But what about marking the *little* things? In the words of English author Samuel Johnson, *"Our brightest blazes of gladness are commonly kindled by unexpected sparks."*

Maybe they're not so little after all...

Think about how you felt the last time you were on the receiving end of an unexpected random act of kindness. Seldom are these acts of monetary significance, and yet their impact and importance can be quite dramatic and far reaching, often with rippling "pay it forward" effects.

Let the unexpected kick-start your complacency and see what happens!:

- Hide notes around the house that your partner will find after you've gone. Or stick a card or note in his/her suitcase.
- Do some of his or her chores without being asked.
- Next time you go out for a nice dinner, call ahead and have them place a single red rose on her plate.
- Go to a comedy club on a *weeknight rec-night*, and laugh the night away.
- Break out the his-n-her aprons, and cook up a new recipe together.
- Arrange to meet your spouse for a tasting at a new wine bar; enjoy some tasty artisan cheese.
- "Take it outside." Dress up an outdoor table and light your fare with the ambiance of tiki torches (or citronella candles if the mosquitoes attend).
- Get out the oil or lotion and give a heavenly foot or shoulder massage, and rub away the stress of the crazy day.

Big relationship paybacks… all at little or no monetary cost. (Challenge yourself to come up with some others the next time you are quieting your mind and stretching your brain – see "Make Time" above!)

◆ Nibble and Hold Hands

"Tis the human touch in the world that counts—the touch of your hand and mine—which means far more to the sinking heart than shelter or bread or wine, for shelter is gone when the night is o'er, and bread lasts only a day, but the touch of the hand and the sound of the voice live on in the soul always."

Spencer M. Free – author

Touch is one of the five senses we use to interpret our world. But while the other four senses are localized in a single area (taste to your mouth, smell to your nose, sound to your ears, and sight to your eyes) the sensation of touch reaches from the tips of your fingers to the bottoms of your feet.

Human skin has hundreds of thousands of submicroscopic nerve endings which serve as tactile receptors to detect temperature, pressure, texture and pain. Workers in hospitals and nursing homes have long been aware of the therapeutic value of a sympathetic touch. There are also significant psychological connections to the impact of touch on things like child development, healing, and anxiety reduction. A lack of affectionate touch has been shown to cause depression, violence, memory deficits, and illness in both humans and monkeys. (There are empirical supports to this, but we're going to keep this section focused on expressive communication, and not turn it into a science journal here!)

Everyone knows that certain parts of the body are more sensitive to touch than others, and you can support your connection and closeness with your significant other by knowing what those are.

- **Earlobe**. It may sound a little odd, but a gentle kiss on your significant other's earlobe, or gently rubbing them with your fingers, is very effective. The skin on the earlobes is thin so the nerve endings are close to the surface, making them more sensitive to touch.
- **Neck**. The sides and back of the neck are highly sensitive to touch. The neck and upper shoulders is also an area where people tend to tighten up and "lock in" their stress. This is why rubbing the neck is so relaxing.
- **Feet and Toes**. There is also a concentration of nerve endings in the soles of your feet and in your toes, which is why standing for long periods of time and/or wearing improper shoes can become quite uncomfortable. Consequently, the feet and toes will respond – most

gratefully! – to massage.

- **Hands.** Our hands are used more than any other part of our bodies for sensing touch. Corpuscles in the fingertips are especially sensitive. Lightly caressing your partner's fingers and hands is both a stimulating and non-threatening way to demonstrate affection.

Remember – these exercises should communicate *care* and *respect*… they are an end in themselves, and not simply a preamble to sex.

◆ Inclusion
"Intimate relationships cannot substitute for a life plan, but to have any meaning or viability at all, a life plan must include intimate relationships."
> *Harriet Lerner* – psychologist

Often I hear couples saying that they don't like to talk about work around the house. They prefer to "come home and leave work at the door." In my opinion, that kind of compartmentalization may have worked for prior generations, but it doesn't for ours. Our generation has *different dynamics* created by two-career households, business travel and technology, which can spur a different kind of angst and relationship stress than when the working world stopped at dinner time.

I believe that it's healthy for couples to share key aspects of their respective days with each other on a daily basis. That doesn't mean belaboring and bemoaning every annoying detail in search of pity or sympathy. Rather, it's relating some of the key challenges and successes of your day, so there is a shared understanding of what you are dealing with. (The same courtesy and caring ear should be extended to your spouse as well – whether he or she works in the professional world or not.) This will keep you connected, and add depth to your understanding and appreciation for each other.

If your career is one that has travel requirements (trade shows, sales meetings, training seminars, etc.) look for opportunities to bring your significant other along. Most companies have policies around spouse travel, but there are usually ways to involve your significant other either before, during, or after an event (on your own dime of course). It will go a long way to help expand your spouse's understanding of what you do in your professional life and feel like part of the team.

◆ Call Daily
"If we all discovered that we had only five minutes left to say all that we wanted to say, every telephone booth would be occupied by people calling other people to tell them that they loved them."

Christopher Morley – journalist and poet

My entire professional career, I have been a "heavy" traveler. My trips have been both domestic and international, and I'm usually gone 40–50 percent of the time. (That's a lot of nights in hotel rooms with uncomfortable beds, "climate control" that *doesn't*, and bathtubs with drains that are backed up with strangers' hair. But I digress….)

One of the areas where I unwittingly added undue stress on the road was the way I handled communication – home.

Over the course of my career, I have traveled with many business associates who have had "loose" tethers with their spouses while on the road. No written itineraries exchanged… and only occasional calls home. Initially,

I believed this was the ultimate sign of trust in a relationship, and it gave them more flexibility in terms of late dinners with customers and drinks in the Holiday Inn bar afterward. So I wanted this same understanding when I traveled… and I played it out to a fault.

My then-wife had trust issues that developed from her prior relationships gone sour. I came to learn (after the fact) that she needed more regular communication with me… at the same time I was wanting more travel autonomy like my colleagues enjoyed. She wanted more… and I was giving her less.

Business travel is hard on you and it's hard on your spouse as well.

Here are a couple of hard-won axioms to make "hitting the road" a little less painful and stressful for you both:

1. **Nothing good ever happens in a bar after midnight**. Autonomy is nice, but prudence is critical. There is no disrespect in telling a customer or other work-mates that you want to call it a night and get ready for the next day. You don't need to be the last dog howling at the moon. Set a sensible limit for yourself, and stick to it.

2. **Where there's mystery, there's mischief… or the fear of it… which can be just as damaging to your relationship.** Let's not kid ourselves. We all know that mischief takes place when people travel and they don't use good sense. Our significant others know this too. And that's why regular contact with your home base is absolutely vital. It shouldn't be perceived as a lack of trust by your spouse… but rather an acknowledgement on your part that the world is full of people with questionable scruples, and you have a caring spouse

at home who is concerned for your well being. Guard against mischief on the road... and don't allow the *fear* of it to creep in and deteriorate your relationship either. Pick up the phone and make those important calls home with a smile in your voice.

Don't allow poor communication when you're traveling to foment unnecessary anxiety. My significant other and I both travel extensively in our careers... me as a business executive, and she as a flight attendant with US Airways. Thankfully we both have an appreciation for the importance of *daily* communication... and *evening* communication too... or our relationship never would have even left the gate.

♦ Annual Living Sprees
"O, how bitter a thing it is to look into happiness through another man's eyes."
William Shakespeare

Shoulda... woulda... coulda. These are words you should make sure to avoid having to use as you move into your golden years. Plan to go on at least one "living spree" with your significant other each year, and hold it sacrosanct. Go someplace you've never been before and enjoy new experiences together and swirl life across your taste buds like a fine wine.

In the words of Benjamin Franklin, *"The U.S. Constitution doesn't guarantee happiness, only the pursuit of it. You have to catch up with it yourself."* Find something that you and your significant other or family enjoy doing, and strategize it collectively. Then map out your "journey" together to help assure that you actually see it through. For instance:

125

- If you're golfers, choose 18 unique golf courses that you'd like to play, and make your own "score card" to complete as you do so.
- If you like domestic travel, agree to visit all 50 states together, and create a map and scrap book to track the places that you've been (something other than a spoon or thimble collection!).
- If you enjoy camping, put together a roadmap of parks that you want to visit, sights you want to see and things you want to learn.

In my case, Bevy and I have decided that we want to visit all of the islands in the Caribbean together. To keep it visible, fresh and exciting, we have framed a map that we can use to plot the islands that we've visited... and lay out our plans for the others. We're also collecting a small amount of sand from each island in an hourglass as a home based reminder of our times on the islands.

Put your "maps," sand, scorecards, photos and park stickers out in the open, and have fun sharing your journey with family and friends!

◆ Tech Respect

"In North America there is the general belief that everything can be fixed, that life can be fixed up. In Europe, the view is that a lot can't be fixed up and that living properly is not necessarily a question of mastering the technology so much as learning to live gracefully within the constraints that the species invents."

Jonathan Miller – British theater director and humorist

In today's fast-paced environment, no doubt you will need to be on the computer, Blackberry or cell phone on a fairly regular basis. But don't allow the "e-raid" bombardment to blow up the time you need at home for personal sanctity and fulfillment. Keep your personal and professional lives from colliding, potentially damaging both. With forethought and discipline, they *can* peacefully coexist together.

There is no defined boundary between your home and your work unless YOU create it.

Be cognizant of respecting your home environment, and use your tech tools with discipline and proper timing. Negotiate blocks of time in your home when you do and don't use your electronic tools. BTW – that goes for the kids and their texting as well. The world won't stop revolving if they put down their cell phones and they aren't texting for a couple of hours each night. LOL.

◆ Emoticon
"Each of us makes his own weather, determines the color of the skies in the emotional universe which he inhabits."
>   ***Fulton J. Sheen*** – Catholic bishop

Emoticon is a portmanteau word formed from the words *emotion* and *icon*. By definition, an emoticon is an arrangement of keyboard characters intended to convey an emotion or the mood of the writer. Some of our newer electronic instruments (like my Blackberry) will now automatically replace the keyboard characters with these small corresponding images.

Emoticons can either enhance or change the interpretation of plain text. Thinking back to the "Mehrabian 7-38-55 rule" regarding expressive communication, it's an electronic way of trying to advance beyond using just words, and adding the expression of tone of voice or body language to the text…(sort of).

127

In western-style writing, we read from left to right. Similarly, western-style emoticons are viewed from left to right. As an example, an emoticon face is built beginning with the eyes on the left... followed by the nose and the mouth. Here are just a few simple examples of some of the more common emoticons. *Hint – If you have trouble visualizing the emoticon, rotate the page clockwise 90 degrees.*

:-)	smile with nose	**: P**	tongue out or joke
:-(	sad face or frown	**: O**	shock or surprise
;-)	wink	**:-/**	annoyed or awkward
: D	grin or laugh		

It's nice to know that every now and then, these electronic tools that tend to take *away* from our relationships can occasionally help us *support* those relationships as well... (again, sort of). An emoticon can never replace the value of a *real* smile or *real* feelings expressed in person, but it can be a fun way to add color and spirit to your prose.

We disproved the notion that work/life balance is an oxymoron or an unachievable state. Balance can be achieved with a smart plan and a little positive energy. It starts with time management and setting priorities to make sure you are putting your energy into those life aspects that really matter most. And it's also about relationship management and expressing yourself fully with your loved ones.

We explored some simple tools to help you in these areas. Use the "Eisenhower Matrix" to get a handle on how you spend your time, and to help you expand your Quadrant 2 activities... those which are important to you and have limited time pressure. And recognize the importance of expressive communication and the greater impact that your actions and behaviors provide, trumping that of the spoken word.

Use the **Executive's Guide to Expressive Communication** to help you connect more fully with your loved ones, and to get maximum relationship value from your time spent with them.

PARTING THOUGHTS

We began this book with an analogy of a little boy who arrived late, panting and sweating after walking his bike to school. When the teacher asked why he didn't ride the bike, he replied, "I was so late, I didn't have the time to stop and get on it."

The point of this book was to help you "get on," and overcome – or at least challenge – the kind of thinking (or lack thereof) that is keeping you sweaty, exhausted, and "late for school." It was about making sure you achieve a passing grade in leadership and career development by putting some useful tools in your backpack to help you... but now it's up to you to pull them out and complete your "homework."

- You now have at your disposal, the "keys of organization" – the *"Control + Alt + Delete"* model to give you the daily structure you need to keep your professional and personal development on goal.

- You have **The Four Controls of Business Leadership** to use as a guide in developing as an excellent leader of character – well suited for the challenges of the 21st century workplace and home.

- You have an understanding of *inertia* and *dominant logic* in business – and how to recognize them and use them to your benefit.

131

- You have an advanced awareness of change (both within and outside of your control) and how to effectively manage it using *Alt* and *Delete*.

- You have a renewed understanding of the importance and rewards of work/life balance for the benefit of both your personal and professional lives...**it's your due.**

- You have the *"Eisenhower Matrix"* and **"The Executive's Guide to Expressive Communication"** to help you solidify the important work/life balance bedrock, giving you a strong foundation upon which to grow – both personally and professionally.

Put these tools to work for you and add *Control* to your life. *Alt* your lifestyle as needed and *Delete* those aspects that can take you off your course.

As for your *professional* side...pick a couple of areas to focus on now...and identify others that you will take on later. Create a personal "board of directors" of trusted friends and associates whom you can rely on for shared counsel, advice and insights.

As for your *personal* side...remember that you had a personal life before your professional life, and you will long after your professional life is over. Make sure you take more than just a 401k with you into your golden years. Life isn't all rainbows and butterflies...it's about compromise. Love is a renewable resource, so make sure you are building on those relationships that matter most in your life. People enjoying genuine work/life balance don't have to be an "endangered species." Tend to the tools and tips we discussed in this book and you will be well on your way.

ACKNOWLEDGMENTS

Although the work of a single author, this book is a collection of life and career adventures – influenced by many. My deepest thanks to the professionals who taught me so much through the years and helped shape my leadership thinking and style.

- Phil Drake, who hired a wide-eyed college kid and taught me the importance of customer sensitivity and the basics of "big business."
- The Kohler family, for allowing me the privilege of learning and developing as an associate on the team not once – but twice!
- Jim Beardsley, whose leadership was most influential as I began to frame the characteristics I would develop and refine during my career.
- Bob Weis, who shared his mastery of organization and critical thinking skills with me.
- Sue Freitag, who kept me "together" through eight years, three jobs, and was both a professional and personal confidante through it all.
- The many wonderful workmates and friends at Pella, Kohler, Master Lock and Grainger I've had the pleasure of growing with through the years. You know who you are!

And deepest thanks to my family and friends for their endless love and support.

- Bob and Jo Howard, my parents, for always being there and for instilling the important virtues and values of life upon me.
- Natalie, for the love, support and understanding that only a daughter can give.
- Beverly, my betrothed, for helping me to hone my "expressive communication" skills and find love again.
- Bruce Morrow, for helping inspire me to write this book and for guiding a first-time author along the way!

And thanks to the team of professionals who helped bring **Control + Alt + Delete Leadership** to life.

- Maggie Brydges, my wonderful editor at "Word Brydges."
- Doug Dillon, for creating the illustrations.
- Marshall McClure and Parke Press for book design and press management.
- Tom Caldart and Moving Pictures Wisconsin for the author photo.
- Troy Tarnutzer and Lisa Sympson for their creative input on cover design.

To all of you whom I have named, please accept my sincerest gratitude.

To all of you who have read this book, best wishes as you develop your skills as a leader of character and balance your success at the office with serenity and enjoyment in your personal life with your loved ones.

ABOUT THE AUTHOR

Ralph Howard is presently VP-Specialty Brands and an officer of W.W. Grainger. With 2009 sales of $6.2B, Grainger is the leading broad line supplier of facilities maintenance products. The Specialty Brands business (formerly Lab Safety Supply, Inc.) is comprised of 10 unique brands with customer focused product lines and services. Some of the brands include Lab Safety Supply, Imperial, Gempler's, Highsmith and McFeely's.

Prior to joining Grainger in 2009, Ralph was President of Canac Cabinets, which was a multi-national Kohler Company business with over 1,900 associates throughout North America. Canac was the largest manufacturer of frameless kitchen cabinetry, serving both the new construction and remodeling consumer markets.

Over the course of his career, Ralph has worked for four blue-chip companies, beginning in 1985 with Pella Windows and Doors in Pella, Iowa. Pella is a privately-held billion dollar corporation well known for producing high-quality windows and fenestration products. He also spent eight years in leadership positions with Master Lock Company in Milwaukee. Master Lock is the world leader in padlocks and security products, and is a unit of publicly-traded conglomerate Fortune Brands.

Ralph worked for Kohler Company twice during his career, amassing over 11 years of combined service. Prior to running Canac, he was Vice President of Sales for Kohler's multi-billion dollar plumbing business, and he was also Vice President and business leader for the Sterling brand. Kohler is the privately-held global leader in plumbing products and power systems. He has built and managed both large and small businesses, and he's been in leadership positions through three significant business turnarounds during his career.

Prior to general management, Ralph worked in multiple disciplines with the previously mentioned companies. He started as a Service Engineer and he advanced through the ranks of marketing, sales and business management.

Academically, he holds a Bachelor's degree in Mechanical Engineering from the University of Wisconsin-Platteville, and he's a Harvard Business School alumnus as a graduate of the prestigious General Manager Program in Boston. He's currently an outside director on the boards of two privately-held companies, and he's the founder of *"Via Leadership, LLC"*. He's a passionate and enjoyable speaker, and he can be reached at **ralph@ralphhoward.com**.

LaVergne, TN USA
14 March 2010
175941LV00003B/5/P